Christ-Centered COACHING

7 Benefits for Ministry Leaders

JANE CRESWELL

CHALICE
PRESS
ST. LOUIS, MISSOURI

Bible quotations, unless otherwise noted, are from the *New Revised Standard Version Bible,* copyright 1989, Division of Christian Education of the National Council of the Churches of Christ in the United States of America. Used by permission. All rights reserved.

Scripture quotations marked (NIV) are taken from the HOLY BIBLE, NEW INTERNATIONAL VERSION®. NIV®. Copyright © 1973, 1978, 1984 by International Bible Society. Used by permission of Zondervan Publishing House. All rights reserved.

Diagram on page 96 adapted and used with permission from *The Heart of Coaching* by Thomas G. Crane, FTA Press—www.craneconsulting.com, 858–487–9017.

Cover art: Getty Images
Cover and interior design: Elizabeth Wright

Visit Chalice Press on the World Wide Web at
www.chalicepress.com

10 9 8 7 6 5 4 3 2   07 08 09 10 11 12

Library of Congress Cataloging–in–Publication Data

Creswell, Jane.
  Christ-centered coaching : 7 benefits for ministry leaders / Jane Creswell.
    p. cm.
  ISBN-13: 978-0-827204-99-7 (pbk.)
  ISBN-10: 0-827204-99-X (pbk.)
  1. Christian leadership. 2. Christian leadership–biblical teaching. I. Title.
BV652.1.C74 2006

253–dc22

2005037499

To my parents,
Franklin and Neva Aiken,
who started me on the journey of following Jesus

and

To the farmer and his wife,
Charles and Peggy Creswell,
who inspired me to become a missionary to the corporate world
while I was a summer missionary.

What a gift it is to have two sets of Christian parents!

Contents

Editor's Foreword

Inspiration and Wisdom for Twenty-First-Century Christian Leaders

You have chosen wisely in deciding to study and learn from a book published in **The Columbia Partnership Leadership Series** with Chalice Press. We publish for

- Congregational leaders who desire to serve with greater faithfulness, effectiveness, and innovation.
- Christian ministers who seek to pursue and sustain excellence in ministry service.
- Members of congregations who desire to reach their full kingdom potential.
- Christian leaders who desire to use a coach approach in their ministry.
- Denominational and parachurch leaders who want to come alongside affiliated congregations in a servant leadership role.
- Consultants and coaches who desire to increase their learning concerning the congregations and Christian leaders they serve.

The Columbia Partnership Leadership Series is an inspiration- and wisdom-sharing vehicle of The Columbia Partnership, a community of Christian leaders who are seeking to transform the capacity of the North American Protestant church to pursue and sustain vital Christ-centered ministry. You can connect with us at www.TheColumbiaPartnership.org.

Primarily serving congregations, denominations, educational institutions, leadership development programs, and parachurch organizations, the Partnership also seeks to connect with individuals, businesses, and other organizations seeking a Christ-centered spiritual focus.

We welcome your comments on these books, and we welcome your suggestions for new subject areas and authors we ought to consider.

George W. Bullard Jr., Senior Editor
GBullard@TheColumbiaPartnership.org

The Columbia Partnership,
905 Hwy 321 NW, Suite 331, Hickory, NC 28601
Voice: 866.966.4TCP, www.TheColumbiaPartnership.org

Acknowledgments

Judi Hayes: This book wouldn't have happened without your help. Thank you very much. You are a talented writer and a delight to work with. I greatly appreciate your friendship, encouragement, and genuine interest in coaching. Thanks for your attention to making this book an inspiration to ministry leaders. Many thanks to Trent Butler, editorial director for Christian Board of Publication, for introducing us.

George Bullard: New ideas need a place to blossom and grow, and you are a genius idea gardener. Thanks so much for believing in me.

My Clients: Thanks for the trust that you've placed in me by allowing me to coach you, and for the education you've given me in the process.

My Coaches: I particularly want to thank Jim Beasley, Dr. Lee Smith, Dr. Jeannine Sandstrom, and Laurie Beth Jones. At some point in time, I remember telling each of you that I couldn't possibly ever do the things you believed that I could. Thanks for not believing me but rather believing *in* me and constantly inspiring me to use God's help.

My Support System: Thanks to: Linda Miller for being the dearest friend, Perry Rhue for uplifting prayers; Ed Allen for memorable adventures, Frank Skidmore for all your support, Teresa Artis for inspiring lunches, Jerry Fletcher for fun collaboration, Neal and Cherri and Candice for being like family, Stephanie and Frank for *being* family even when I disappeared from the scene at times, Bryan and Andrew for your words of encouragement that came at just the right times and for making me such a proud mom, and my husband, Tom, my true love.

Thank you, Lord. May you be the one glorified.

CHAPTER 1

Why *Christ-Centered* Coaching?

One of the scribes came near and heard them disputing with one another, and seeing that he answered them well, he asked him, "Which commandment is the first of all?" Jesus answered, "The first is, 'Hear, O Israel: the Lord our God, the Lord is one; you shall love the Lord your God with all you heart, and with all your soul, and with all your mind, and with all your strength.' The second is this, 'You shall love your neighbor as yourself.' There is no other commandment greater than these."

MARK 12:28–31

Love the Lord your God with *all your strength*. Wow, what a daunting task! A little thought about it may at first evoke more questions than answers. What exactly does it mean? How do you love the Lord with strength?

Surely strength as it's used here doesn't mean muscle. If so, many of us are in big trouble! With our limited physical ability and endurance, most of us wouldn't have much love to give if loving with all our strength meant muscle.

But if the meaning of *strength* is expanded to include all the gifts, talents, skills, personality traits, cognitive preferences—all the characteristics that contribute to making each individual a unique being created in God's image—then that's a concept each of us can embrace. Yet even that expanded definition of strength continues to lead to questions.

How can you know what your strengths are—all those gifts, talents, skills, personality traits, cognitive preferences—all those bits that are uniquely you? That process could take a lifetime to explore and discover. You can take an endless variety of assessment tests to gain some awareness and understanding of all those characteristics, but then what would you do with all that information?

What if you change over time? How would that affect loving God with all your strength? Would your love for him change, too?

And what about that word *all*? That would mean you couldn't love God with all your strength if any part of you—your gifts, talents, skills, personality traits, cognitive preferences—didn't unite in loving God. That would mean that you have no gift; no talent; no part of personality; no left-, right-, front-, or back-brain activity that isn't dedicated to loving the Lord.

Sounds overwhelming, doesn't it? But Jesus didn't offer the Great Commandment as an option. It's not a choice. It's a command.

You as a ministry leader probably know well the overwhelming feeling of working out of all your strength—loving God and loving others. The pressures in the church today are tremendous. At least, that's what current statistics and ministry leaders themselves are saying. Let's take a look at the current state of the local church in the world today.

What's the Problem?

In the United States today church membership is declining in most denominations. Individual attendance is declining, as well as the number of hours individuals are willing to give to the church each week. Many ministers conduct a lot more funerals than baptisms and weddings in their churches. When worship leaders look out across their congregations on Sunday morning, many see a lot more wrinkles and gray hair than squirming youngsters and whispering teenagers.

That congregational mix and their dedicated time and money mean fewer lay leaders to carry the load. Many of the faithful are getting too old to teach active children or identify with teenagers and young adults. As the leaders of the past are dying off, fewer adults in succeeding generations are stepping up to take their place.[1]

Among the younger adults who do attend, fewer are willing to commit to the demands of the jobs they are asked to do. Teaching Sunday school means not only hours of weekly preparation but also a commitment to attend every Sunday. Serving on committees or teams often means long hours of meetings and little real ministry. Program organizations of the past just don't inspire young adults to commit to such leadership positions. Every year it's harder for churches to fill the jobs template with adults who will say yes.

And then we face the challenge of those outside the church. If people inside the church struggle with the church's value and relevancy in their own lives, for many outside the church it's not even an issue.[2] In fact, many people today are turned off by Christianity! They find it—or at least their image of it strongly influenced by the media—arrogant, judgmental, and archaic.[3] Yet Jesus, in addition to the Great Commandment, left the church with the Great Commission—go, teach, baptize (Matthew 28:18–20). That means telling the unchurched about their need for a Savior in ways that they can hear it and actually attract them to a relationship with Jesus Christ. Many church leaders find themselves exhausted with their seemingly futile attempts to rally the flock, frustrated by the demands of aging buildings and bodies, desperate to meet a budget, and overstressed by congregational and community demands. In the face of all this, many ministers are deciding to seek easier ways to earn a living.[4] They especially choose an alternate path if it means more time with family and less stress over seemingly impossible tasks and a lack of answers to impossible challenges.[5]

Why Are So Many Churches and So Many Ministers Facing These Challenges Today?

The mix of causes is probably unique in every situation. The many reasons given for the state of the church and ministry today include:

Postmodernism—The postmodern environment has changed our culture.[6] People with this mind-set question everything. They are not automatically ready to consider the Bible to have absolute truth, for they think much of truth is relative. They demand interactivity, and that includes learning, worship, and ministry activities.[7] Giving money so someone else can go to Africa makes no sense to them. Sitting in a meeting when they could be painting a widow's house seems pointless. Will the church have to write off people of a postmodern mind-set? The church has endured two thousand years of cultural changes that were as challenging as this one, yet it has persisted and grown. No, I don't believe that postmodernism alone can be the cause for the state of the church today. While it may contribute to the downfall of some churches, many will survive the transition as they shift some of their approaches to worship, ministry, missions, and Christian education. Those who make the transition well will thrive in this changing era.

Lack of leadership—The church not only faces a postmodern era but also one that has lost its zeal for denominationalism or even Bible knowledge.[8] The average adult in the pew has limited understanding of the polity of the church or its denomination and probably little interest. Few systems for teaching the Bible are actually geared toward the ways in which adults learn effectively. These deficits lead to struggles, misunderstandings, and hurt feelings when discussions arise about membership and leadership expectations and requirements. As a result, those who are willing to lead are often unqualified and untrained.

Lack of leadership has often put even more responsibility, time demands, and frustration on ministers. Add to that the idea many laypeople have that ministers were hired to do the work of the church, and they, the members, should not be expected to take on such demands on their time, energy, or finances.[9]

Ultimately, the demand on ministers is to cast a vision that will inspire members to follow, committing their resources to join in reaching the goals to make the vision a reality.[10] Then those who respond to the vision must be taught, equipped, trained, motivated, and encouraged. Somewhere along the line, this breaks down in many churches and adds to the pressure on many pastors and staff ministers.

Untapped potential–Perhaps the adults in your church aren't just lazy or undisciplined, lacking commitment. Perhaps many are loving with something less than all their strength–living in the "not-all" state; they haven't yet determined to love God with all their strength. They may not know how. They may not know how their gifts, talents, and skills can be used in ministry. They may hear the sermon on Sunday but have a total disconnect on their role in the Kingdom–on Sunday, Monday, or any other day. They may dwell on the edge of the Kingdom but have no idea how they could make a contribution to it.

What will it take for laypeople to get a vision of their role as Christ's followers in terms of ministry both inside and outside the church? What more would it demand from ministers today? Aren't most ministers in the "all" state, giving everything they've got in service and love for God and his people? Maybe, maybe not. Untapped potential abounds in laypeople and ministry leaders alike.

Unrealistic expectations–While laypeople often aren't living up to the expectations of ministers, clearly ministers get feedback that they are often not living up to the expectations of their church members.[11] When you felt called to ministry, did you ever dream that you would be dealing with some of the tasks and situations– even nightmares–that you're dealing with today? That's one of the reasons some ministers have had enough and are leaving the church. Their calling just didn't include the things that consume their time.

Many ministers are caught in an endless morass of administrative chores, "fire-fighting," maintaining programs that seem to have lost their energy if not their purpose, and responding to unhappy and needy members. By Sunday they confess that they are just going through the motions. They find themselves in the "not-all" category during worship–the part of their call they value most. Rather than compromise worship and their high calling, many abandon ship.[12] And many who remain in ministry confess feeling more frustration and less joy in ministry than ever before.

Unworthy goals–Has your church ever spent more time and energy than it should on any of these issues: the color of the walls or the carpet, whether to rent or purchase a photocopier, the wording that goes on the church sign, or whether to sponsor a student ski trip? Even more important issues can bog the church down in endless discussion: which curriculum to use, where youth will go on a mission trip, whether to share space with an ethnic or foreign-language congregation, or how to respond to current denominational controversies. Sometimes the harsh words and hurt feelings last a lifetime and seem to negate the ministry goals that began the discussion.[13]

What If?

What if many of these negatives could be turned around?

What if laypeople were to move from the "not-all" to the "all" state? What if their untapped potential could be harnessed and used in Kingdom ministry? What if they became motivated, enthusiastic, totally committed?

What if the church could unite in using its limited resources together in meaningful, focused ways? What if church members began to see results, to get excited about what the church was doing and accomplishing? What if what they experienced in church just kept getting better and better, totally living up to their expectations and engaging them in fulfilling ministry?

What if the structure, the programs, the ministries of the church were organized in a way to maximize the gifts, talents, skills, personalities–the *strengths*–of both ministers and laypeople so that all were united in a common God-given vision?

What if the Great Commission and the Great Commandment became the driving forces for both ministers and lay leaders so that secular people were being attracted to Christ and all members were growing as disciples, united in love for God, for one another, and for those outside the church?

What if this change occurred not only in your church but in churches throughout your community, your city, your state, the nation? What then could be accomplished for the Kingdom?

What if your church could change? What if your ministry was more often than not one of joy and fulfillment? What if you had dedicated, motivated, equipped leaders lined up waiting for Kingdom assignments?

What if all of this could happen where you are right now?

How Will This Book Help?

Right now, for most ministers and most churches, a large gap separates the reality and the "what-if" columns. While most ministers would like to rewrite those ledger sheets, they probably think it's impossible. If you are experiencing any of these frustrations, you're probably thinking:

> Yes, but my situation is different. You have no idea what I've been through, what I'm going through. You can't imagine what some of my members are like, what they have done, what they have said to me, how uncommitted, ill-equipped, unmotivated, and helpless they are. You just don't know how difficult, how impossible, this situation is. I can't possibly turn it around. There's no way it can improve. I see no way out but to move or leave the ministry.

Unfortunately, such thoughts, while honest, do little to help the situation.

Tapping the potential pool

Coaching can help.[14] This book has been developed from wide experience in coaching in both the secular and the church context. Many of the principles developed here come from secular coaching experiences. However, the unique focus of this book is applying the strengths of coaching philosophy and practice to Christian experience: the needs of the church, its ministers, and its members. With examples from Scripture referenced frequently, I want to point out opportunities for exercising *a specific type of coaching–Christ-Centered coaching.*

Many of the things that I describe throughout this book as benefits of *Christ-Centered* coaching are also benefits of coaching in general. I have not really put forth the effort to point them out because this book is intended to educate, support, and inspire coaching that is Christ centered.

Christ-Centered coaching focuses on tapping into that great pool of potential in your church. George Bullard uses the phrase "full Kingdom potential."[15] It's available in your church. People in your church can move from the "not-all" to the "all" category in loving and serving God. Don't you want to be there and be a part of tapping into all the skills, talents, gifts, personalities—strengths—lying dormant in your church right now? *Christ-Centered* coaching can help you see this dream come true. Coaching can help you become the key to making it happen in God's own way.

Christ-Centered coaching is a customized approach to conversations between two individuals who trust God to be a partner in the conversation. I often call myself a "customized adult-learning partner." A coach can help you discover insights in yourself and your own situation that you never dreamed possible.

Christ-Centered coaching is effective at an organizational level as well as at an individual level. Coaching skills can also be applied to work with groups, committees, and teams for the good of the whole. And through your own coaching experience, you will learn to use these skills with others—one-on-one and in group situations.

Focusing on root causes

Coaching goes beyond surface troubles, whatever they are, to focus on the root cause. Often, the root issues are completely unknown. They lie buried deep inside you. Once revealed, you can learn to deal with, overcome, or channel them.

Some common coaching topics include personal and organizational purpose/mission/vision, leadership development, succession planning, organizational effectiveness, stress management, and barriers to full commitment—just the issues that many ministers are facing in churches and even denominational leadership positions today.

Coaching really fits with the postmodern mind-set. In this relational one-on-one approach, the person being coached—you—will discover your own issues and needs, focus on your concerns, and find your own answers. Coaching offers no package deals, no right answers, no preconceived results. In the process of this experiential dialogue, you will work out of your own way of thinking and operating. This will occur in your personal life and in your ministry. In short, coaching will help you find and address all those things that were potential root causes to the problems you are experiencing. Don't read this to say that coaching advocates a self-sufficiency in which God is not needed. In reality, it is quite the opposite. *Christ-Centered* coaching often causes ministry leaders to renew and deepen their dependence on and relationship with Jesus Christ.

Based on real-life scenarios

To help you see the benefits of coaching, this book will provide real-life scenarios. Some of you may think when you read them that you know exactly who I'm writing about. But you don't, so don't even try to guess their identities. Over the years, I've had a role in either coaching or delivering coach training to more than five hundred ministry leaders. Each scenario is based on a combination of a number of people in ministerial roles who have faced similar situations and had similar experiences and discoveries in the coaching process. In fact, you will surely see yourself in a number of these situations. That's why they're included–to help you see the many benefits of *Christ-Centered* coaching in situations much like yours.

Even in cases in which the experiences described are different from your own, hopefully you will still be able to see how coaching is relevant to a variety of experiences–those you've had and those you are yet to have. The coaching skills portrayed in the scenarios are written at an Associate Certified Coach (ACC) level of coaching competency. That is the first level of coach certification with the International Coach Federation (ICF).[16] The purpose of writing at that level is to model results that can come from a coach who has had coach training and some experience, while also showing you that a coach does not have to be at a mastery level to produce good results.

Confidentiality is at the foundation of coaching.[17] No one's confidentiality is betrayed in this book, and no good coach would ever betray a client's trust. That can't be emphasized too strongly. These stories are real, but in a way they are everyman and everywoman. They are drawn from real life but not from one life. Easily identifiable characteristics have been changed, but the principles remain. These very human stories will touch your heart and soul because they reflect people who have walked where you walk today, often in situations they found frustrating at best and hopeless at their worst.

Who Is the Author?

And finally, who is Jane Creswell, in many ways a product of the corporate world, that I should attempt to help you in a ministry situation? Let me tell you just a little about my own personal journey.

As a summer missionary in college, I worked with migrant children. I noticed that some were very responsive, and some were difficult to reach. On further investigation, I noticed that those who responded well were attached to farms where the farmer had a reputation for being kind and compassionate to his workers. Those who were unresponsive came from farms where the conditions were harsh and the farmers were taskmasters. I believed the same results would be found in the business world, and that summer I felt God's call to be a missionary in the corporate world. This meant loving God and loving people with all my strength in an environment in which God is often ignored or unwanted. Of course, my self-proclaimed missionary status was unofficial and largely unknown by those with whom I worked.

Ultimately, my corporate experience led to my becoming the first internal coach at IBM and founder of IBM Coaches Network.[18] On this particular part of my journey, I learned a lot about coaching executive leaders and creating a coaching culture within organizations.[19] But my credentials are not only based on that experience. I have also studied coaching and earned the Master Certified Coach distinction from the International Coach Federation. That translates into more than twenty-five hundred contact hours of corporate coaching prior to June 2003.[20]

I spent several years watching corporate executives respond positively to coaching experiences, even turning around their components or businesses. They found the workplace a healthier, more rewarding place for themselves and for those who worked with them. After these experiences I was invited to apply the same coaching skills in the church environment with ministry leaders in both the church and denominational settings. At first I was reluctant. Having been involved in a church all my life, I have a very high regard for pastors, other ministers, and denominational leaders. I wondered how, coming from a corporate world, I could help them—if indeed they actually needed any help.

Now, after working with church leaders for several years, I understand that ministers, like corporate leaders, deal with similar needs and root causes of frustration. And more than ever before, I am convinced that the approaches of coaching apply and can help people in all walks of life. The difference between the corporate world and the church is the eternal significance of their goals and purposes. Nothing is more important than following the commands of Jesus in the Great Commission and the Great Commandment. And *Christ-Centered* coaching, I'm convinced from my own experience, can help you love God—and love people—with *all* your strength.

CHAPTER 2

Christ-Centered Coaching

What It Is and What It's Not

For surely I know the plans I have for you, says the LORD, plans for your welfare and not for harm, to give you a future with hope. Then when you call upon me and come and pray to me, I will hear you. When you search for me, you will find me; if you seek me with all your heart, I will let you find me.

JEREMIAH 29:11–14A

What a difference a lunch can make!

This morning Tom sat in his office and stared at the books on his shelves. He was so stuck that he couldn't even figure out what to do with his time today. How did he get to this point? When he became a pastor at age twenty-four, he was excited and full of enthusiasm. He loved sermon preparation, delving into the Scriptures, reading books about each text, listening for the Holy Spirit's guidance. It was pure joy! He looked forward to years of quiet time in his study preparing sermons, and hours spent with individuals and groups, helping them to grow as followers of Christ.

Fast-forward twenty years later to now. Whatever he has been experiencing, it certainly hasn't always been joy. Just this morning he was wondering, *When was the last time I entered my study with an untroubled mind to focus on God's Word and what God wants me to say on Sunday?* All he seems to be doing these days is attending endless committee meetings in which nothing is ever accomplished. Some days he thinks he needs a striped shirt and a whistle because he's developed real skills as a referee, settling angry disputes among members. Or maybe he could become a firefighter, having put out a lot of fires lately—or at least trying to.

But now, after lunch, Tom's thinking his situation is not so bad after all. Maybe there is a glimmer of hope. He had lunch with his friend and confidant, Ed, who is an executive coach. Ed is a great listener! He seems genuinely to care about Tom and his challenges. No matter what's going on, Ed listens as if Tom's woes are as important to him as they are to Tom.

Funny, all he did was listen, ask some really good questions that helped Tom think through a plan for getting unstuck, and Tom left lunch knowing exactly what to do next and ready to get it done. In only an hour or so, Tom is back in his study refreshed, with an action plan, and ready to tackle the afternoon.

Yes, that definitely was a good lunch!

Tom had plenty of strength that wasn't being used staring at books. But with the day-in, day-out drudgery his ministry had become, he felt exhausted and trapped. Tom had within him the untapped potential to deal with the day's activities; he just needed someone—a coach—to help him find that untapped potential within himself. Helping Tom find the untapped potential within himself to know what he needed to do that afternoon was just the first step. With Ed's ongoing help, Tom began to see that he had untapped potential that went beyond getting through each day productively. He discovered that he had untapped potential to revisit his calling to ministry, to reevaluate where his church and his life and ministry were going, and to make some changes so that he once again could feel that he was making a difference in people's lives—a Kingdom difference, an eternal difference. Once again Tom was finding significance in the life he was leading.

Tom's situation reflects two ways *Christ-Centered* coaches can help:

1. They can help a person on a micro level find his or her untapped potential to make each day productive, to move from being stuck to having a plan for dealing with day-to-day activities and to see at the end of the day where something has been accomplished; progress has been made.
2. They can help a person on a macro level rediscover his or her focus/call/purpose and move toward leading a life of significance.

Sometimes the person being coached is stuck in only one of these levels, the micro or the macro. Sometimes he or she may be stuck at both levels.

During that "good lunch," Tom felt like he was chatting with a trusted friend. That friend who listened well and asked just the right questions—who helped him turn a dead-end morning into a refreshing, productive afternoon—was actually using the skills of a coach. Although it wasn't evident to Tom, Ed—having heard Tom's heart—was gently guiding Tom through a process. The process was designed to help him discover his untapped potential so that he could feel good about what he does each day. The process helped him once again find joy in doing what God called him to do.

This scenario shows an informal coaching relationship in which coaching skills are used but a formal coaching relationship has not been established. This type of coaching relationship is common for ministry leaders to have with those they lead. We'll see examples of more formal coaching relationships between a ministry leader and a coach in later chapters.

Christ-Centered Coaching Is...

Coaching focuses on promoting discovery. *Christ-Centered* coaching additionally utilizes the power of the Holy Spirit in that discovery process. By helping you focus on the untapped potential within you, a coach can guide you to discover that potential and what needs to be done. The coach won't provide the answer, make decisions for you, or tell you what to do.[1]

Finding answers, not providing answers

Coaches will help you find answers rather than provide answers for you. Unlike Job's friends who had all the answers, a coach will listen and ask questions to guide you in finding the right answer for you. Have you ever tried to talk with a friend about your situation, but you found as well-intentioned as your friend was, all she or he wanted to do was "fix it," to suggest the solution so the problem would go away? And you left the conversation more frustrated and feeling misunderstood. That's not the way a coach works. You may find, for the first time in your life, that someone is really listening to you, that someone really understands you.[2] And in that process you will begin to find the answers you need.[3]

A coach will help you find untapped potential within yourself—whether that means getting through the day productively or setting a new, or redirected, course to help you know that your life is making a difference, that you are indeed fulfilling God's plan and purpose for your life.[4]

A coach is dedicated to helping you. You alone are the focus of his or her attention when you are together or talking on the phone.[5] This isn't one-size-fits-all problem solving. It isn't even small-group education and fellowship. It's one-on-one, customized learning. Each minute of coaching is for you alone.

Coaching is done through a predictable set of skills, models, and competencies.[6] While the coach's methods may not be obvious to you, the results will be. Often a coach's process is all but invisible because a skilled coach thinks about you and your needs and focuses entirely on you. You'll be amazed when your coach asks just the right questions to help you find just the right answer. It's no accident! That's what the coach is trained to do.

Definition of Christian Coaching

Christ's Vision and Mission

+ Scriptural Principles

+ Christ's Presence

+ High Standard of Excellence as Trained Coach

_____

= CHRISTIAN COACHING

Building a confidential relationship

Wherever you are, your coach will walk along beside you in relationship. Often it's difficult for a minister to admit having any needs. It's difficult to let someone help; after all, you're the one who helps others. Part of the difficulty is the perceived risk. The last thing you want is for your staff or congregation to know that you are struggling. They may have guessed it, but you certainly don't want to confirm it. With a coach you don't need to worry. Everything you say will be held in strictest confidence, so this truly is a relationship you can trust. By the way, your staff and congregation will probably notice; but what they'll notice is the positive change in your demeanor, your attitude, your productivity, and your focus.

The best image for coaching is a vehicle.[7] The word *coach* derives from an old British word meaning "horse-drawn carriage." You can think of the coaching process as a journey, one in which you are caught up in the process as you move toward a specific, targeted destination. The coach's goal is to help you find direction and enjoy the ride!

While you are being coached, *you* make the choices. You'll decide where you want to go; the coach will help you get there. The coach can tell you in advance little about the journey but only what the coaching process will be like; the details about the journey will unfold as you engage in the experience.

Tom Bandy says, "Christian coaching in the postmodern world needs to step beyond the boundaries of control established by past Christendom. Openness to mystery, receptivity to the irrational and unexpected, and readiness to be seized, shaken, and stirred by an ultimately unknowable God are not virtues in which Christendom churches normally excel."[8] That mystery of the unexpected is a fabulous journey that a *Christ-Centered* coach will help you experience.

Christ-Centered Coaching Is Not...

Coaching is not a replay of high school football! Even the term *Christ-Centered* coaching might elicit fears of judgment and reprimand. Nothing could be further from the truth. No one is going to be yelling at you to make a certain play. No one except you is going to be critiquing your performance. There are no laps or pushups for failure to execute the coach's commands. No one is going to tell you what the next play is or even what your goal is. Making the coach or the team look good is not the goal, though it may be a side effect.

With your coach, you'll design the plays, and you'll choose the plays to execute. You'll analyze your own behavior. And you'll determine whether and when you succeed.

Not counseling, consulting, or mentoring

Christ-Centered coaching is not counseling, consulting, or mentoring. It's not therapy. A coach is not a "man with a plan" who has gone before you and knows whether "the plan" works or leaves disaster in its path. A coach is not someone who wants to create little clones of himself or herself because, "If it worked for the coach, it will surely work for you."

In consulting and mentoring, the expertise lies in the consultant or the mentor and is transferred to the person. In coaching, on the other hand, the expertise lies within you, the person being coached. The coach's role is to help you discover how to use more of your own potential and how to determine a strategy for which expertise is needed that doesn't already exist.[9] Counseling is about resolving how the past informs the present, while coaching is only about the present and moving forward. Counseling assumes a lack of health, while coaching assumes health. The goal is to put your valuable skills, gifts, talents, and personality to work–maximizing your strength to do what God wants you to do.

There's a reason people commonly confuse coaching with these other helpful professions. Coaches, counselors, and consultants all use some similar skills. They are all good at observation and at asking questions. People are often more familiar with counselors and consultants, but may have limited experience or understanding of professional coaches. Coaches may have similar skills, but they show a difference in their perspective and in the application of those skills. As you continue to read, the differences, though perhaps sometimes subtle, will become increasingly clear to you. As the differences are more and more apparent, you'll see how important it is to distinguish those differences.

Over time your coach may also become your mentor and your friend. The combination of coaching–prompting discovery in you– and mentoring–filling in some information from experience that you don't have–can be a powerful combination.

Biblical Tenets of a *Christ-Centered* Coach Approach[10]

Just as some counselors and consultants are Christian–and some are not–so also some professional coaches are Christian–and some are not. And some Christian counselors, consultants, and coaches do not choose to work out of a Christian worldview.

Make no mistake, my worldview is Christian, and my coaching is centered in Christ. Many of the people that I coach in corporations do not share that worldview. Nevertheless, we are able to work well together in the coaching relationship to help them realize their potential and achieve their goals. When it comes to being coached myself, I have worked with a number of coaches, and I prefer to have a *Christ-Centered* coach with a Christian worldview. The Kingdom perspective is essential for me, and I believe it is essential for you as a ministry leader.

Throughout these pages you will find Scripture references and biblical allusions. The Bible is full of models for good *Christ-Centered* coaching. You'll learn more about that, too, as we go along.

Not long ago I led a Sunday school class in which we took the life experiences of the participants and all of us thought of a Scripture that applied to a particular person's experiences that week. Then I asked the person coaching questions related to that Scripture. It was a powerful experience for everyone involved, especially the coach! I have found Scriptures that remind me of each of the following tenets of a *Christ-Centered* coach approach. After each Scripture I've used the respective approach to develop the questions included in this section. These are examples of how a coach might use Scripture to help the ministry leader move forward.

1. *Christ-Centered* coaches assume untapped potential in everyone and insist that it be discovered and developed.

■
You are wonderfully made:

> I praise you, for I am fearfully and wonderfully made.
>   Wonderful are your works;
> that I know very well.
>   My frame was not hidden from you,
> when I was being made in secret,
>   intricately woven in the depths of the earth.
> Your eyes beheld my unformed substance.
> In your book were written
>   all the days that were formed for me,
>   when none of them as yet existed. (Psalm 139:14–16)

COACHING QUESTION: How can more of your "wonderfulness" be lived out?

■
You are a child of the Creator:

> But to all who received him, who believed in his name, he gave power to become children of God, who were born, not of blood or of the will of the flesh or of the will of man, but of God. (John 1:12–13)

COACHING QUESTION: What would be different if you embraced the potential of "being a child of God" more fully?

■
God gave humans dominion over all the earth:

> God blessed them, and God said to them, "Be fruitful and multiply, and fill the earth and subdue it; and have dominion over the fish of the sea and over the birds of the air and over every living thing that moves upon the earth." God said, "See, I have given you every plant yielding seed that is upon the face of all the earth, and every tree with seed in its fruit; you shall have them for food. And to every beast of the earth,

and to every bird of the air, and to everything that creeps on the earth, everything that has the breath of life, I have given every green plant for food." And it was so. (Genesis 1:28–30)

COACHING QUESTION: What would it look like for you to demonstrate "dominion" in your current challenge?

■
God has a plan for you:

For surely I know the plans I have for you, says the LORD, plans for your welfare and not for harm, to give you a future with hope. Then when you call upon me and come and pray to me, I will hear you. When you search for me, you will find me; if you seek me with all your heart, I will let you find me. (Jeremiah 29:11–14a)

COACHING QUESTION: What are the plans God has for you? If you don't know, what else can you do to "seek with all your heart"?

■
Hope, riches, and power are at your disposal:

With the eyes of your heart enlightened, you may know what is the hope to which he has called you, what are the riches of his glorious inheritance among the saints, and what is the immeasurable greatness of his power for us who believe, according to the working of his great power. God put this power to work in Christ when he raised him from the dead and seated him at his right hand in the heavenly places, far above all rule and authority and power and dominion, and above every name that is named, not only in this age but also in the age to come. And he has put all things under his feet and has made him the head over all things for the church, which is his body, the fullness of him who fills all in all...

   I pray that, according to the riches of his glory, he may grant that you may be strengthened in your inner being with power through his Spirit, and that Christ may dwell in your hearts through faith, as you are being rooted and grounded in love. I pray that you may have the power to comprehend, with all the saints, what is the breadth and length and height and depth, and to know the love of Christ that surpasses knowledge, so that you may be filled with all the fullness of God.

Now to him who by the power at work within us is able to accomplish abundantly far more than all we can ask or imagine, to him be glory in the church and in Christ Jesus to all generations, forever and ever. Amen. (Ephesians 1:18–23; 3:16–21)

COACHING QUESTION: What could you do to live in hope, riches, and power as Paul describes?

___

The power of the Holy Spirit is at your disposal:

"You will receive power when the Holy Spirit has come upon you; and you will be my witnesses in Jerusalem, in all Judea and Samaria, and to the ends of the earth." (Acts 1:8)

COACHING QUESTION: What would your ministry look like with even a little more access to the power of the Holy Spirit? What about a lot more?

2. *Christ-Centered* coaches focus on identifying and strengthening strengths.

___

Each Christian has a job to do:

Indeed, the body does not consist of one member but of many. If the foot would say, "Because I am not a hand, I do not belong to the body," that would not make it any less a part of the body. And if the ear would say, "Because I am not an eye, I do not belong to the body," that would not make it any less a part of the body. If the whole body were an eye, where would the hearing be? If the whole body were hearing, where would the sense of smell be? But as it is, God arranged the members in the body, each one of them, as he chose. If all were a single member, where would the body be? As it is, there are many members, yet one body. (1 Corinthians 12:14–20)

COACHING QUESTION: If you were using your full Kingdom potential, what would your role be in the body?

Whatever you've been given, make the most of it:

"For it is as if a man, going on a journey, summoned his slaves and entrusted his property to them; to one he gave five talents, to another two, to another one, to each according to his ability. Then he went away. The one who had received the five talents went off at once and traded with them, and made five more talents. In the same way, the one who had the two talents made two more talents. But the one who had received the one talent went off and dug a hole in the ground and hid his master's money. After a long time the master of those slaves came and settled accounts with them. Then the one who had received the five talents came forward, bringing five more talents, saying, 'Master, you handed over to me five talents; see, I have made five more talents.' His master said to him, 'Well done, good and trustworthy slave; you have been trustworthy in a few things, I will put you in charge of many things; enter into the joy of your master.' And the one with the two talents also came forward, saying, 'Master, you handed over to me two talents; see, I have made two more talents.' His master said to him, 'Well done, good and trustworthy slave; you have been trustworthy in a few things, I will put you in charge of many things; enter into the joy of your master.' Then the one who had received the one talent also came forward, saying, 'Master, I knew that you were a harsh man, reaping where you did not sow, and gathering where you did not scatter seed; so I was afraid, and I went and hid your talent in the ground. Here you have what is yours.' But his master replied, 'You wicked and lazy slave! You knew, did you, that I reap where I did not sow, and gather where I did not scatter? Then you ought to have invested my money with the bankers, and on my return I would have received what was my own with interest. So take the talent from him, and give it to the one with the ten talents. For to all those who have, more will be given, and they will have an abundance; but from those who have nothing, even what they have will be taken away. As for this worthless slave, throw him into the outer darkness, where there will be weeping and gnashing of teeth.'" (Matthew 25:14–30)

COACHING QUESTION: What one thing could you do to maximize what the Master has given you?

■

God will renew your strength:

> But those who wait for the LORD shall renew their strength,
>> they shall mount up with wings like eagles,
> they shall run and not be weary,
>> they shall walk and not faint. (Isaiah 40:31)

COACHING QUESTION: What would define "waiting on the Lord" for you right now?

3. *Christ-Centered* coaches look at people and the organization/ church/ministry as possibilities for constant reinvention.

■

You are a new creation:

> So if anyone is in Christ, there is a new creation: everything old has passed away; see, everything has become new! (2 Corinthians 5:17)

COACHING QUESTION: What needs to pass away?

■

God will renew a right spirit within you:

> Create in me a clean heart, O God,
>> and put a new and right spirit within me. (Psalm 51:10)

COACHING QUESTION: What would it take for you to adopt God's new perspective on this topic?

■

You must be born again:

> Jesus answered him, "Very truly, I tell you, no one can see the kingdom of God without being born from above." (John 3:3)

COACHING QUESTION: What one shift would get you closer to seeing the kingdom of God?

■

You can change and become like a child:

> "Truly I tell you, unless you change and become like children, you will never enter the kingdom of heaven. Whoever becomes humble like this child is the greatest in the kingdom of heaven." (Matthew 18:3–4)

COACHING QUESTION: If you look at your situation with wonderment, fully trusting and only considering the cares of the day, like a child, what would you see and what would you be prompted to do differently?

■

Your renewal comes through the Holy Spirit:

> But when the goodness and loving kindness of God our Savior appeared, he saved us, not because of any works of righteousness that we had done, but according to his mercy, through the water of rebirth and renewal by the Holy Spirit. This Spirit he poured out on us richly through Jesus Christ our Savior, so that, having been justified by his grace, we might become heirs according to the hope of eternal life. The saying is sure.
>
> I desire that you insist on these things, so that those who have come to believe in God may be careful to devote themselves to good works; these things are excellent and profitable to everyone. (Titus 3:4–8)

COACHING QUESTION: Since the Holy Spirit living through you is not limited by what you've successfully accomplished before, what new, excellent, and profitable works might the Spirit be leading you to do?

4. The success of the *Christ-Centered* coaching experience extends through you to other people and activities.

■

Go and make disciples of all the nations:

> Now the eleven disciples went to Galilee, to the mountain to which Jesus had directed them. When they saw him, they worshiped him; but some doubted. And Jesus came and said to them, "All authority in heaven and on earth has been given to me. Go therefore and make disciples of all nations, baptizing them in the name of the Father and of the Son and of the Holy Spirit, and teaching them to obey everything that I have commanded you. And remember, I am with you always, to the end of the age." (Matthew 28:16–20)

COACHING QUESTION: What is a specific action that you could take to move from thinking and talking into "going"?

Coaches start with you where you are and build from there:

"You will receive power when the Holy Spirit has come upon you; and you will be my witnesses in Jerusalem, in all Judea and Samaria, and to the ends of the earth." (Acts 1:8)

COACHING QUESTION: Where are you now, and where does God want you to be? How can you plan the steps to get there?

Tips for *Christ-Centered* Coaches

- What do you say when someone asks you what coaching is? Practice being able to explain to them in a brief and compelling way. Maybe this is a little too obvious, but you could let them read this book to know the benefits.
- Demonstrating coaching to someone is one of the best ways to help people understand what it is.

Tips for Working with a *Christ-Centered* Coach

- Think of a time when you were prompted to discover an answer instead of being given the answer for a difficult challenge. What can you take from that experience to help make being coached a positive experience?
- Try discovery questions on someone else—a child, a friend, or a ministry colleague. Notice how they respond. Were they frustrated in not receiving an answer or inspired by the one they discovered? How might your responses be similar or different? How can you use this experience/insight to make being coached a more productive experience for yourself?

CHAPTER 3

The Benefits of
Christ-Centered Coaching

The purposes in the human mind are like deep water, but the intelligent will draw them out.

PROVERBS 20:5

Charles was the pastor of a relatively large church (500+ attending Sunday school). He had been at the same church for twenty years. Over the years he had earned respect beyond his own congregation, and people across the state recognized his name and appreciated his leadership. He was frequently asked to take on regional leadership roles in his denomination, and often served as a guest conference leader or speaker.

If you asked other pastors in the area to name a pastor who was a "success," many would have put Charles at the top of the list. His congregation loved him. He was well respected in his state. He enjoyed collegial relationships across denominational lines. He had a great family life with kids who were growing and making him proud. Life was good, and Charles would be the first to admit it.

But while Charles had achieved a certain level of success, he wasn't quite content. He was good at what he was doing, but he'd been doing it so long the challenge was gone. Charles was wondering: "What's next? I have a lot more years of ministry in front of me. Is

God calling me to use my successful experience to have greater impact for the Kingdom?"

In his first coaching session, I asked him, "Where are you, and where would you like to be?"

Charles was quick to respond: "In most people's eyes, including my own, my ministry is successful. There's no conflict in my church. Things seem to be going well in my church and my region. I guess that's where I am and where I want to be."

"Really?" I probed for more, "You are living your full Kingdom potential?"

A more thoughtful, honest answer this time: "Well, I have been wondering if there is something more that I could be doing, somewhere I might have more impact, something more that God wants me to do."

Orienting around Strengths

As we began to explore whether Charles was loving God "with all his strength," Charles realized that he enjoyed writing, but seldom found time for that anymore. He was spending about twelve to fifteen hours a day on church- and ministry-related work. And he was increasingly challenged to give his family the time they wanted and deserved—and that he wanted to give them. He just didn't see how he could find the time to write.

"Tell me more about your strengths as a writer," I encouraged.

"In college and seminary my professors gave feedback that I was able to give good examples; reduce complex topics into simple, understandable language; and include humor that wasn't derogatory or at anyone's expense. I'm not sure if that's really anything special. A lot of people going through a D. Min. program probably have that level of skill and ability—if not greater."

Remembering that he said he wanted to focus on finding the time to write, I said, "And maybe not. Writing may come so naturally to you that you don't even have to work at it. Maybe that's a top strength for you, and we should focus on helping you use it to full Kingdom potential. How can you find the time?"

At first, Charles thought that was a crazy question. He'd already said he didn't have enough hours in the day. "You can't just create more time, you know. I don't know where I could find the time."

Clarity and Focus

"What are you currently doing that is not having as much impact as sharing the successes of your twenty-year ministry at this church with others?" I asked.

"That's a great question! Before I give you an answer, I just have to say I really like that question! I haven't asked myself that question in a long time. In fact," he laughed, "it sounds like something I would ask someone else but don't really ask myself. I actually do want to be a person of impact, and I'm not holding myself to that standard." Charles thought a minute before he went on. "That's more of what I want to talk about—having a greater impact. Now, let me try to answer your question.

"When I think about the possibility of expanding my ministry beyond my congregation and my state, by writing about experiences that might benefit others and help them in their ministry, well, there are plenty of things that I do every day that are less important than that. For one, I spend lots of time going to committee meetings where I don't think I'm really needed. And some of those committees don't accomplish much anyway. They meet for ninety minutes, and usually only about fifteen of the ninety could be called productive. But most of those meetings are in the evenings. If I didn't go to those, I'd probably choose to spend more time with my family over writing."

"How could you do both?" I asked, "Spend more time with your wife and children and also find time for writing?"

Charles mentally ran through the list of committees. After some thought, he determined that he could begin with one committee. He believed he could stop attending those meetings without jeopardizing the work of the committee or his relationship with the committee members. But almost as quickly as he had determined to take this course of action, he began to wonder again whether they would think he wasn't doing his job if he started missing these committee meetings. What would people think? What would they say? His concerns—fears, really—quickly popped to the surface.

"What strategy can you develop to communicate this change in how you choose to spend your time—a strategy that people will see positively?"

Confidence

Charles winced, hesitated, and then said, "Well, I guess I could be really open and explain my reasons for not coming." The minute those words were out of his mouth, he realized that if he felt like time was wasted, others might feel the same. He decided to explain his reasons and at the same time offer to help the committee figure out ways to have more impact and reduce the frequency and length of the meetings to the benefit of everyone involved. That kind of change would be a win for everyone!

In our next coaching session, Charles reported that the committee gave him a round of applause for helping reduce the number and length of their meetings—even the committee chair! It turns out that everyone was thinking the same thing, but no one, except for Charles, had had the courage to say anything about it.

He was excited about spending more time with his wife and kids. They had already noticed a difference in his schedule just by his changes in working with that one committee.

Learning

Charles was so pleased with the way this committee had responded that he began to wonder what would happen if he could help all the committees in a similar way. Then he wondered if anyone else had done this before and whether other ministers might like to hear how he had approached this situation and made this positive change in his life and in the lives of his members.

"How can you find out?" I asked.

He began to think and list. "I could ask some friends in regional offices. I could see if any of the periodicals I receive have addressed this issue. And at a conference not long ago, I met an editor from a publishing house. I think he would give me some pointers if I called him. In fact, I remember that he had information about a writers conference he was doing. I didn't pay much attention at the time."

"Which of these ways best fits with your way of learning?" I asked

"I think I'd like to pursue this from several different directions. So, I guess—all of them."

Intentional Progress

Charles did talk with others as he had planned. He found that while a lot was being written about churches doing away with committees, or transitioning committees to teams, not a lot had been written about making committee meetings more productive or about the pastor's involvement or about how frequently some committees really need to meet. But the team concept really intrigued him. In a lot of ways, that sounded like the next step for what he was beginning to do with the committees at his church.

He gathered literature about team ministry. He liked the different model, the ministry focus; and he thought his people would like it too.

Charles was right. The more he talked about team ministry, the more excited both he and his congregation became. They felt that their time was better spent, more productive, and more about ministry than administration. Charles hadn't seen energy like this in his church in a long time. Teams were actually looking for jobs to do, people to help, rather than sitting in meetings and wasting time. This team concept was pulling people together, giving them focus and direction, and reaching new people, too. Community concerns were being addressed, and the church was growing again.

But Charles hadn't lost his goal of finding time to write. He had even more to write about than before. He could see that many churches would be moving to the team concept, and he already had a smooth transition and positive experiences to share. He just knew that the process his church used would help others, and his church's success could allay some fears of other ministers about this big change in church operations.

Coaching Others

Charles also began to notice that his own way of relating to committees and teams was changing. Before, he was often the silent partner or the expert on the team. But his behavior was changing, largely as a result of his own coaching experience.

He began to ask questions in meetings. He listened intently to what the people were saying. And he saw that his questions were not seen as threats but as tools to move the meeting and the ministry along. People were leaving committee and team meetings excited, talking about how productive the meeting was and the ministry their team was doing now and planning to do in the future. Laypeople were accomplishing more than they ever had before—with commitment and enthusiasm. Some of the very people who had accepted little responsibility in the past were stepping up to the plate, and some who had done little but grumble and groan were now productive team members. The longer this continued, the more he realized that the teams didn't need him all the time. Once they caught a vision for where their team fit in the church's overall ministry, all they had to do was work out details. They seemed to enjoy having that responsibility and accountability. They knew he was available if needed, so they didn't feel neglected. They were busy with their ministry, and he was busy with his!

God-Sized Goals

Eventually Charles was able to find two hours a week for writing articles that could be published in denominational publications on church health. This was something that before he would have considered almost impossible, because it would take a miracle for him to have more time with his family and find time to write. Charles was beginning to feel that there really was more that God wanted of him and God had been faithful to help him get to a whole new level in his ministry.

He had never expected so many benefits from his coaching experience. Now he believed without any doubts whatsoever that God had created the desire in his heart to do more and had used a *Christ-Centered* coach to help him move forward. Now he was wondering what other exciting ministries God had in mind for him!

Charles was ready for *another* next level.

What Are the Benefits of *Christ-Centered* Coaching?

Charles, over time, experienced almost all the major benefits of coaching. This is the case with many people but certainly not all. Some people are stuck and need help in only one area. Others, like Charles, just keep benefiting from the experience.

1. Orienting around strengths

First Charles discovered that he had untapped potential. He had strengths that he had discounted or neglected and not put into use. That meant he really wasn't loving God with all his strength, and perhaps that could have been what prompted his desire to explore opportunities for expanded ministry. Coaching helped him discover those unused strengths and search for ways to use them. With a coach's help, Charles "leveraged his strengths for full Kingdom potential."

2. Clarity and focus

When ministers, and even churches, lose their focus–their vision or purpose–they often end up involved in denominational politics. Whatever the current hot issue is, it begins to consume their time and energy.[1] Because the pastor/minister/denominational leader has lost focus for the ministry he or she is called to do, politics begins to take the focus. *Christ-Centered* coaching helps redirect that focus on ministry.

Charles was able to help his committees abandon their administrative, discussion-driven meetings and turn to a team ministry approach that focused on results.[2] People were being helped, lives were being changed, participants felt energized, and the church was growing. *Christ-Centered* coaching helped Charles see new possibilities and to focus on new approaches to ministry, to clarify the task, and to arrive at better ways to do the work.

3. Confidence

When Charles first began to consider making some changes, his first thoughts were full of fears: *What will people think? What will they say? What will they do?* Not changing seemed a lot safer in many ways; after all, things were going pretty well. Why rock the boat?

But as he began to think through a way to make his first change positive for all concerned, he determined that he would go through with his plan in spite of his fears. That small change was so well received and so positive for everyone that he gained confidence and continued to suggest changes. Without the fears dragging him down, he began to see more and more possibilities. He was energized by all the positive actions taking place in his own life and ministry. Every day he felt that he was discovering new possibilities, creating new ways of doing ministry. His life and ministry were being transformed.

4. Learning

Frankly, it had been a long time since Charles felt that he had really learned anything new, taken any risks, charted any new course, challenged the status quo, or felt any adventure in ministry. Of course, he went to conferences and heard what others were doing. He might come home with a tidbit of an idea to implement. But he had never been a big believer in seeing what worked well somewhere else and then just copying that in his own church.

With the help of a *Christ-Centered* coach, Charles found himself in the middle of self-directed learning customized just for him. He and his coach focused his interests, his strengths, and his desires to expand his ministry—and Charles found ways to make that happen. He set his own personal goals, guided by how he was being led by the Holy Spirit, and—together with his coach—explored ways to reach them.

5. Intentional progress

Nothing is more encouraging than success. Charles began having success in his personal goals—to spend more time with his wife and children and to write—as well as in his ministry at church. Step-by-step, he saw progress in achieving his goals.

With his coach's help Charles closed the "knowing versus doing gap." He'd known since seminary days that writing came easily for him and was something he enjoyed, but he'd never done anything about it. With an intentional plan, worked out with his coach, he moved toward his goal. With the coach's help he found time he thought he didn't have. With an intentional plan his two goals moved from impossibility to reality.

With encouragement from his coach, Charles designed a way of making himself accountable to himself, to do what he set out to do. He hadn't thought about writing in years. That strength lay dormant and hidden. Who knew if it could live again? If he thought about it at all, he might have decided it was a silly idea and that he had little to offer. Having a *Christ-Centered* coach made the difference. His coach listened, affirmed, asked meaningful questions, and kept confidences. Because of the trust they developed in their relationship, he wanted to be accountable. That made all the difference.

6. Coaching others

Charles didn't enter a coaching relationship to help him with his church ministry or his ministry relationships. He felt pretty good about how all that had worked through the years. He didn't begin the process because his life had problems.

However, he learned a lot from his coaching experience—far more than he dreamed. He experienced having someone really listen to him, asking questions to cause him to go deeper into his own strengths and behaviors, helping him find untapped potential within himself that took him by surprise. The whole process was so affirming and empowering for him that without even thinking about it, he began to use some of his coach's skills with the people around him. The basic skills were similar to what he had learned in seminary years ago, but they were delivered in a way that was well beyond anything he had learned in seminary or even in conferences since then. They seemed to fit some of the postmodern folks he'd been trying to move into leadership positions. These postmoderns responded positively as well. His relationships had never been better. His staff and lay leaders felt affirmed, and he was grateful to help others experience some of the benefits of *Christ-Centered* coaching that he had realized.

7. God-sized goals

When Charles first met with his coach, he began by saying how good his life and ministry were. He wasn't there because things weren't going well; he didn't really have any complaints. But radical changes would take a miracle, he thought. He was out of time, and he just didn't see any way that he could do anything more.

His church was doing well. Yes, it could do better. But he had learned through the years just how much to expect of people. Unrealistic expectations of laypeople just led to frustration.

But *Christ-Centered* coaching changed all that. He was more focused, more energetic, and accomplishing more than he had dreamed he could. He had expanded his personal ministry through writing. And his church had greatly expanded its ministry by engaging more and more laypeople in ministry. Younger leaders were being mentored. People were involved, and more were being reached. God's vision for the church had never been clearer, and lives were being transformed for the Kingdom.

No, Charles's life wasn't perfect. He still had to deal with conflicts in the church. He still had to work hard to envision the future of the church and to communicate it to church leaders and members. He still had to deal with, and help others deal with, the dynamics of change. But he faced these challenges with more confidence and a more positive perspective.

Who would have believed that time spent with a *Christ-Centered* coach could open so many doors and accomplish so much?

How Do Benefits Relate to One Another?

Each person in a coaching relationship has an experience that is unique. Because it is one-on-one, focused on the individual, no two experiences are exactly alike. However, they do tend to move through fairly predictable stages of benefits. Everyone doesn't experience all of them, as Charles did. But most people do experience multiple benefits. Even though subsequent chapters will focus on single benefits, the benefits are tied together. We will move through the benefits in the order they have just been presented here, the most common way people tend to experience them. You might want to envision these benefits as a wall or a pyramid, with the benefits building on top of one another in the order described.

Benefits of Coaching

Coaching Others		God-Sized Goals	
Intentional Progress			
Clarity/Focus	Confidence		Learning
Orienting around Strengths			

Discovering your *strengths* is foundational. It's hard to make headway at all without knowing them and leveraging them. Finding untapped potential is the first step for most people. Then comes orienting your life around knowing what your strengths are—ordering your days to use them fully.

Clarity/focus, confidence, and *learning* come next for most people. *Clarity/focus* is generally a piece that is missing and an immediate place where a coach can help. Everyone has confidence issues. Those who don't—or say they don't—may not be working toward God-sized goals. And everyone has fears to overcome; they vary depending on the individual, but everyone has them. Learning to strengthen your strengths and deal with your fears allows you to continue to move forward in new ways. Approaching life as a learner instead of a person who already knows all they need to know is a natural outgrowth of gaining clarity and focus and confidence.

Intentional progress comes next. As a result of coaching, you can begin to build momentum at this point when the other benefits are being realized. Because of an effective coaching experience, you will actually develop habits for yourself, based on your coaching experiences, and establish new patterns of behavior to achieve your goals.

Coaching others is a natural progression of receiving all the other benefits. You will want others to experience what you've experienced, and at this point the benefits start to be multiplied.

God-sized goals are the highest benefit and most often result from the foundation built as the other benefits—strengths, clarity/focus, confidence, learning, and intentional progress—are realized. If, however, the benefits on the bottom are not fully realized, you will find it much more difficult—but not impossible—to get to the benefits on the higher levels.

From my experience this seems to be almost a predictable order of benefits. If that's the case, this discussion of benefits can also be helpful to coaches to gauge where you are in the coaching experience. The person being coached sets the agenda for the conversation, so I'm not talking about the coach's being directive. It's just helpful to know that this is a likely progression of benefits. Noticing these benefits as they happen informs the context for the *Christ-Centered* coaching relationship.

Key Shifts in *Christ-Centered* Coaching

From telling to asking

Christ-Centered coaches don't tell you what to do; they ask questions. You can see a similar shift from the Old Testament to the New Testament. In the Old Testament the prophets *told* the people; they proclaimed the word of the Lord, giving the people the message God gave them. Jesus' style was entirely different.[3] Notice how frequently he asked questions. He responded to questions with a question. And often those questions probed beyond the surface issue the person raised. The gospels record more than 150 questions that Jesus asked.[4] What I love about Jesus' questions is that I have a different answer each time I read them. I've always changed, hopefully growing in spiritual maturity, since the last time I've read them, so his questions continue to move my growth forward. For me they are powerful enough for a lifetime. I find myself studying them to help me hone my skills as a coach.

Another biblical example is found in the Book of Job. In Job's misery his friends came to him. They had all the answers: Curse God and die! And did that help Job? Not really. He just felt worse with every visit. But when God finally spoke to Job, he asked Job questions: "Where were you when I laid the foundation of the earth?" (Job 38:4). For most of four chapters (38–41), God asks Job questions. And in chapter 42, Job answers God in humility and is satisfied.

From surviving to thriving

As you begin to experience the benefits of *Christ-Centered* coaching, you will begin to experience less stress and more joy. You will begin to experience life to the fullest, as God intended you to live. This, too, has biblical support:

> And this is my prayer, that your love may overflow more and more with knowledge and full insight to help you to determine what is best, so that in the day of Christ you may be pure and blameless, having produced the harvest of righteousness that comes through Jesus Christ for the glory and praise of God. (Philippians 1:9–11)

> Because your steadfast love is better than life, my lips will praise you.
> So I will bless you as long as I live;
> I will lift up my hands and call on your name. (Psalm 63:3–4)

From bondage to freedom

The *Christ-Centered* coaching experience will free you to experience life to its fullest. The more self-understanding you gain, the more you experience the benefits, the more freedom you will feel to do what God has called you to do.

> For freedom Christ has set us free. Stand firm, therefore, and do not submit again to a yoke of slavery…For you were

called to freedom, brothers and sisters; only do not use your freedom as an opportunity for self-indulgence, but through love become slaves to one another. (Galations 5:1, 13)

Now the Lord is the Spirit, and where the Spirit of the Lord is, there is freedom. (2 Corinthians 3:17)

You can trace this thread of freedom in the story of God's kingdom people, his chosen ones. The Israelites suffered in bondage under Pharaoh until God sent Moses to lead them out of Egypt. Even the exodus did not free them of their own fears. Eventually, fear and unbelief led to forty years in bondage in the wilderness before they finally made it to the promised land. Believers know, of course, that we experience ultimate freedom only in redemption through Jesus Christ.

A Biblical Basis for *Christ-Centered* Coaching

The writer of Proverbs wrote, "The purposes in the human mind are like deep water, / but the intelligent will draw them out" (Proverbs 20:5). That's what coaching is all about. That's what coaching does—bring out the depths of your purposes.

Tips for *Christ-Centered* Coaches

- Basic coaching skills come in two categories: input skills and output skills. Input skills include listening, observing, and receiving insights from the Holy Spirit. Output skills include asking powerful questions, encouraging, giving concise messages.
- Study the questions Jesus asked. You'll see some amazing patterns emerge in how Jesus asked the question based on the person to whom he was talking. Some of his most intriguing questions do not have recorded answers. Asking ourselves the questions that Jesus asked others is a powerful way for us to let Jesus "coach" us even today.
- Go back through each scenario in this book. Highlight only the words of the coach. Then think of three other questions or statements that you could pose in that part of the conversation to make the coaching session stronger. This will help hone your skills and help you see that there's always room for improvement.

Tips if You Are Working with a *Christ-Centered* Coach

- Interview coaches to find the best coach for you. Look for someone who has specific training in coaching skills. (Some people don't define *coaching* the way it is defined in this book, so you may want to check on their definition.) Look for someone who has experience in coaching others. (Most coaches can tell you how many hours they have spent coaching people.) Look for someone with certification in coaching (and check out the organization doing the certification for credibility).

- Find a *Christ-Centered* coach. Determine if the coach shares your worldview. Determine if there is anything else that the coach needs to have in experience or credentials for you to have a trusting relationship with that coach.

- Ask for a sample coaching session. The industry standard is that coaches will do a free sample session as a part of an interview. I recommend people interview with at least three coaches before making a decision. Notice how willing you were to participate in the session with each person and how the Holy Spirit spoke to you during the session. The best coach for you will be someone you connect with immediately, someone who will come alongside to help you achieve your full Kingdom potential. The best coach for you *will be a* Christ-Centered *coach.*

- Think about what you will say when your coach asks you what you want to talk about. To prepare for that question, think about any area of your ministry or life in which there is a gap between where you are and where God wants you to be.

CHAPTER 4

Christ-Centered Coaching Leverages Your Strengths

I love you, O LORD, my strength.
The LORD is my rock, my fortress, and my deliverer,
my God, my rock in whom I take refuge,
my shield, and the horn of my salvation, my stronghold.

PSALM 18:1–2

After spending just a few short years after seminary in a local church ministry, Bill was tapped for denominational service. Now, after twenty-five years, working for his denomination was virtually the only ministry he knew or felt he had known. He had loved every minute of it. He had quickly moved into management. He was a good manager and a good leader. He knew how to plan a budget and make it work without compromising the work or jeopardizing the advancement of his employees. He was a good problem solver and almost always found the best win-win solution. Others recognized his work through the years, and he had quickly moved up through the ranks.

Unlike some of his peers who lost their ministry focus, Bill had consistently felt that he was right at the heartbeat of ministry, doing just what God wanted him to do. But gradually he began to notice a change—at least in his attitude. He was silent in meetings instead of helping a group find solutions. He wasn't so quick to respond to his employees' concerns. Some days he thought that if he heard one more rumor about denominational politics he'd start screaming.

Bill had been known for his level head, upbeat personality, and consistent compassion and encouragement. Now an occasional sarcastic remark slipped out, reflecting his increasingly jaded outlook. He wasn't sure what he could do. Bill didn't like the place his attitude had gone. After all these years he actually felt that, in spite of his success, God might be calling him into another ministry. He thought he might like to get outside the building, more in touch with church leaders. But he couldn't imagine how that would happen. The denomination tended to label people. He maintained a good reputation, but it fit a certain niche. Then Bill decided to contact a coach.

As a result of his *Christ-Centered* coaching sessions, Bill soon discovered that he had become very good at what he was doing, but he had to use many skills that were not part of his strength base. He also discovered that he had strengths he had not used in many years. As he discovered more of his strengths, Bill spent time thinking about the best ways to use them in ministry. He decided he needed to start by getting back in touch with people in the churches. Bill began to volunteer for trips to small meetings, to visit in churches—often trips no one else wanted to do. He heard what people were saying. Back in the office, with his influence, he was able to make changes. The momentum built for the effectiveness of the changes he suggested.

He felt energized and enthusiastic again. His reputation as an idea man grew. People began to see him as a creative source rather than a problem solver. His peers raised their eyebrows and asked, "Who knew old Bill could do this?" The changes he suggested proved so successful that they actually hit the secular news media, bringing positive coverage to his denomination. Bill felt ten years younger and eager to continue his ministry journey, helping pastors and churches and his beloved denomination.

What Are Strengths?

Think about strengths as what you are born with, as opposed to skills, which are acquired and layered on top of the strength base. Strengths are talents, gifts, abilities, personality preferences, and cognitive preferences. Strengths are so much a part of who you are that you may have difficulty identifying them. They are so basic to who you are as a human being that you may assume everyone has these strengths. At some points in your life, you will be surprised to learn that your set of strengths is unique to you. They are so inherent in who you are as a person that you may tend to discount them and not even see them as assets that enable you to accomplish a number of different types of work or ministry.

Skills, on the other hand, are acquired. You begin building skills on top of your strengths, even though they may be unknown, almost immediately after birth. You will continue to build skills on top of your strength base for four or five years, until about the time you begin school. Children at play are building skills, layering them on top of strengths.

My husband, Tom, and I have two sons. When they were pre-schoolers, they spent their playtime in different ways. Now that they are older teenagers, we can see how their strengths played a role in their choices. They came wired knowing that they loved to do certain things, and they began immediately building skills on the strengths they were born with. In their preschool playtime, they were passionate about their choices. They didn't care if they fell down or got dirty. They just wanted to follow those curiosities.

Then an external force came along that interrupted that process—school (see "school" arrow in diagram on p. 43). One purpose of school is to build a standard set of skills regardless of an individual's strengths. Some of the skills you acquire in school build on top of strengths, and others don't. Those skills built on top of strengths might be the ones people identify as their favorite subjects. Sometimes people jump to the conclusion that they can tell which skills are built on top of strengths and which are not based on the grades they made in those subjects. That is a fallacy! Intelligent people can choose to learn, to acquire knowledge and skills. They can make good grades in skill areas that are not built on top of strengths. The school does not know how each person is wired. The purpose of basic education is to provide life skills to help everyone function as an adult.

What happens after school in the afternoons? Strengths begin to take over. When you get a chance to choose what you do with your spare time, you build skills on top of strengths. If your mom forces you to take piano lessons, that does not count!

A similar thing happens in college. The model here again has an erroneous assumption. Not everyone builds skills on top of their strengths in college. Whether that is the case depends on how you chose your course of study. People might choose to start with a college degree that has nothing to do with any of their strengths. This can happen if you chose a degree because that's what your parents wanted for you or to achieve a certain income level. But let's just say you picked a degree program that fits your strengths. You might be building skills on top of them, but you would still be adding skills required to get a degree that has nothing to do with your strengths. Still, during your spare time, you will choose to spend your time as a volunteer or in hobbies or sports or activities that revert back to only building skills on top of strengths.

Now let's talk about your career, another big external force Again, you may not even start your career with a job that uses skills built on top of your strengths. That might depend on what jobs were available, for example. In a best case scenario, however, you will start a career that you think fits with your strengths and is in line with who you are. In your career, then, you would start building skills on top of your strengths.

But then what happens? You might start to ask, "What do I have to do to get a bigger church?" That could cause you to veer away from building skills exclusively on top of your strengths. Then you might ask, "What would it take for me to move into denominational ministry?" That might mean more skills outside the realm of your strengths. You could continue asking what you have to do to achieve increasing levels of success—however you define success. When this is the case, you can get yourself into building skills further and further away from your strengths for various reasons until it almost becomes a train you cannot get off. You got on it, and you do not know how to stop the train because you keep building and building and building. You can keep acquiring skills that have nothing to do with your strengths. Contrary to popular belief, you do not realize what you are doing, because you can still learn to do many things well enough to excel in them, even though they are not built on your strengths. You keep acquiring skills and doing them well, and so it is easy to think that those skills are all serving you well.

You may even feel a lot of satisfaction from those skills you are acquiring, even if they are not built on your strengths. This satisfaction, however, is often temporary. Generally, only the skills built on strengths yield long-term satisfaction.

What Difference Does It Make?

Let's look at why all of this matters. First, notice the left-hand side of the model, where many skills are built on top of strengths. Some holes or "skills gaps" still remain on that side of the model. Let's say your job or ministry actually requires you to use mostly skills built on top of your strengths. If those are the skills needed for your job and a challenge happens, as it always does, what would be your response?

Usually your response would sound something like: "I don't know how to do that, but I want to learn." You may say something like, "Great, I love a good challenge. I need to learn some new things; that keeps life interesting." Or, "I have to pick up some skills to do that, but I really want to try something new." Or, "I can see this future for me if I acquire this skill." You might respond in these or in a variety of other ways, but basically the answers people give when their job is in that zone are varieties of "yes!" All their answers sound like, "Yes, I am ready to step up to that challenge."

You can know who is living life and doing ministry in their "zone," because anyone can observe and know. People who are working in the zone give evidence of joy, happiness, and an ability to give back.

But what happens when a challenge happens and your job requires you to use skills that are not built on top of your strengths? Generally people try to be civil, but the responses in this area sound like, "Isn't that somebody else's responsibility?" Or, "I'm not sure that challenge fits with the overall strategy of our organization." It can also be masked as, "I am already working many hours a week; what additional resources are you going to give me to meet this challenge?" These answers are subtle, but all of them sound like "no."

Certain observable behaviors are outcomes of being out of your zone as well. They are stress, physical illness, and being a drain on the ministry, church, or organization. People who are working entirely

Strengths vs. Skills Model

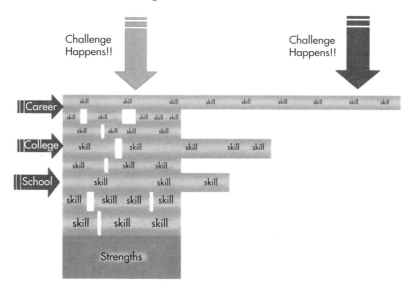

out of acquired skills that weren't built on their strengths don't have an ability to give back. In fact, the opposite is true. People in this situation are taking from the organization.

Have you ever seen this behavior displayed? Have you ever lived it?

How a *Christ-Centered* Coach Can Help

Discovering your strengths on your own isn't always easy.[1] Beginning with school, we are forced to acquire a set of skills that someone else determines we need. The focus is often on helping us improve the skills we don't do well rather than celebrating and helping us excel in the skills we do best—those built on strengths. This pattern often continues throughout education and even into calling and career. A pastor, for example, has to do a large variety of things—preaching, teaching, visiting, managing, counseling. Few people do all these things well. What often happens is that we spend more time and aggravation on what we do poorly, and every skill is pushed to mediocrity. We find little or no time to do our best in the skills based on our strengths because we are spending so much energy trying to improve in our weakest areas. To make matters worse, because they are weak areas, it takes more energy and time to actually see any improvement.

Benefits of Coaching

Coaching Others		God-Sized Goals
Intentional Progress		
Clarity/Focus	Confidence	Learning
Orienting around Strengths		

One of the benefits of working with a *Christ-Centered* coach is that you can look at your life with the backdrop of this model and determine if there is a gap between the situation you are currently in and where you want to be. In a coaching relationship, you will identify your strengths and begin to orient your life and career around strengthening your strengths and leveraging them. Don't expect a coach to diagnose and prescribe, however. Your coach will rather be joining you on a path of discovery.

Most of the time, when people understand this model, they ask, "How do I find out what my strengths are?" You have several ways to do this. Some of my favorites are: High Performance Patterns

(Dr. Jerry Fletcher),[2] The Highlands Ability Battery,[3] and Strengths Finders.[4] Two other ways to find clues to your strengths don't involve an assessment tool, just some observation skills.

To explain this idea, I'll use an analogy of the chemical makeup of our bodies. If you could find out the chemical makeup of your body and plot the amounts in a bar chart, the chart would reveal some small amounts of phosphorus, calcium, and many other elements. A much taller bar would indicate the high amount of water in your body. Imagine doing that with the strengths you were born with. Some of the bars representing your strengths would be lower than average; some would be at or maybe above average; and some, probably only a few bars, would be extremely tall, even off the chart in comparison to others.

Each one of us has a unique set of a small number of strengths that are way above average. These strengths—I call them "top bars"—come so naturally to you that instead of seeing them as strengths, you think that all human beings were born with them. You come to this conclusion because you hardly have to work at developing these strengths. Your coach can tell you the strengths that he or she observes in you. A *Christ-Centered* coach's affirmation and encouragement can help you recall when others have affirmed you and when you felt totally in sync in your work or ministry. But since you think all human beings were born with this same strength, you usually will not believe your coach. I usually have to tell someone four to six times the strengths I observe before the person will accept the fact that his or her strengths are anything special.

You can also gain clues to your "top bars" through self-observation. Since you erroneously think all human beings were born with your strengths, you become frustrated with them if they don't display the behaviors that fit with your "top bar" strengths. A good way to determine your strengths is to start noticing what irritates you about how others operate. You might find it fascinating. Instead of being an irritant, it is a fun process to embrace those top bars as strengths and orient your life around them.

Once you identify your strengths, you can determine how you have acquired skills on top of them. You will probably discover where you have been working in skills not based on your strengths. You may find gaps between what you are doing and what you can do. You may discover that you need to redirect your energies in some ways. You may discover that you need to add some new skills to fill the gaps in your strength-based skills portfolio. And every step of the way, your *Christ-Centered* coach will encourage you and keep holding the vision of what your life can be—even when you can't see it. I know because of George Bullard. Being the coach that he is—though he was never formally my coach—George believed that Jane Creswell could teach coaching skills to ministry leaders, even when I didn't. He held the vision and believed in it and in me before it became reality.

As you turn from spending your time using skills that hang out over the void and redirect your energy to using skills with a solid strength foundation, you will find renewed joy and energy. You will again be in touch with your call. You will find that you are moving from surviving to thriving. You can then become an even greater Kingdom servant, fulfilling the purpose to which God has called you.[5]

In 1994 Jack Nicholson received the lifetime achievement award from the American Film Institute. At the lifetime achievement awards, Nicholson said, "I love what I do and can't believe that they would pay me to do this!" That's the type of joy we should be showing, so that the world will be attracted to us. When the world is attracted to us and we are thriving, the world will be attracted to our God.

Strength from the Word

One thing that distinguishes *Christ-Centered* coaching from any other kind of coaching is looking at strengths through the lens of Scripture. Scripture has much to say about the topic of strength. If you only look at a concordance of an English translation, you'll find many references to *strength,* as well to as *strengthen, strengthening,* and *strong.* Scripture has even more to say on the topic if you go beyond a concordance to study biblical personalities who did or did not orient their lives around their strengths, even noticing their inconsistencies in doing so. We can learn much about God in learning what his Word says about strength. Here are some key additional thoughts on the topic of strength.

Attribute your success (strength) to God:

> When the LORD your God has brought you into the land that he swore to your ancestors, to Abraham, to Isaac, and to Jacob, to give you—a land with fine, large cities that you did not build, houses filled with all sorts of goods that you did not fill, hewn cisterns that you did not hew, vineyards and olive groves that you did not plant—and when you have eaten your fill, take care that you do not forget the LORD, who brought you out of the land of Egypt, out of the house of slavery. (Deuteronomy 6:10–12; see also Deuteronomy 8:1–20)

It is easy for both the coach and the ministry leader being coached to get caught up in taking credit for using strengths in new ways and forget who gave the strengths in the first place. Remembering that God is the Creator of the strengths helps you give the appropriate praise and acknowledgment for them. It also causes us to consult with our Creator more readily to understand what our strengths are when they seem hidden.

Keep in check the concept of strengths:

Let the same mind be in you that was in Christ Jesus,
> who, though he was in the form of God,
>> did not regard equality with God
>> as something to be exploited,
> but emptied himself,
>> taking the form of a slave,
>> being born in human likeness.
> And being found in human form,
>> he humbled himself
>> and became obedient to the point of death—
>> even death on a cross.
> Therefore God also highly exalted him
>> and gave him the name
>> that is above every name,
> so that at the name of Jesus
>> every knee should bend,
>> in heaven and on earth and under the earth,
> and every tongue should confess
>> that Jesus Christ is Lord,
>> to the glory of God the Father.
>>>> (Philippians 2:5–11)

When we know what our strengths are and orient our ministries around them, humility may be even more of a struggle. Remembering Jesus' model of humility becomes even more needed.

Remember that apart from God you can do nothing:

"I am the vine, you are the branches. Those who abide in me and I in them bear much fruit, because apart from me you can do nothing." (John 15:5)

Strength alone is not sufficient for life. The real formula for life as a follower of Jesus Christ is constant connection to him as our source of strength. It is almost impossible to perceive a beginning or an end to this connection. You are abiding.

Acknowledge the source of your strength (resilience):

> I love you, O LORD, my strength.
> The LORD is my rock, my fortress, and my deliverer,
>> my God, my rock in whom I take refuge,
>> my shield, and the horn of my salvation, my stronghold.

(Psalm 18:1–2)

Tips for *Christ-Centered* Coaches

- Use the strengths versus skills model, and ask your clients where they are on the model and where they want to be. They'll know; you won't have to tell them.
- Follow up with helping them focus on the steps to get there.

Tips for Working with a *Christ-Centered* Coach

- What are your strengths?
- How close are you to knowing *all* your strengths? What will it take to discover them?
- Start making a list of all the times you are frustrated by someone. Is there a pattern to these frustrations that could be pointing to your strengths? What specifically would you have to do to embrace these strengths and use them to love the Lord instead of being frustrated that others don't have them?
- What is the definition of loving the Lord with *all* of *your* strengths?

CHAPTER 5

Christ-Centered Coaching
Provides Clarity and Focus

For now we see in a mirror, dimly, but then we will see face to face. Now I know only in part; then I will know fully, even as I have been fully known.

1 Corinthians 13:12

Susan felt as though she needed a new camera. The one she used to note the highlights of what was going on in her life had developed a warped picture of her life. That camera made the picture of her life look like images in the distorted mirrors of a carnival sideshow. When she reviewed recent snapshots of her life, the images bounced back as scattered, unproductive, and stressful. Susan's life was out of focus, and she didn't think she could ever measure up to her own expectations—much less anyone else's—or see the end of her frantic ministry.

Susan was a denominational leader, working at her denomination's national headquarters. She was overwhelmed with her job. She was stretched in so many directions that she didn't really have any idea whether she was making headway in anything.

It wasn't that she was unproductive. In fact, she was phenomenally capable and productive. Because she was, her supervisors and colleagues constantly sought to involve her in every new project.

She knew people all over the nation and beyond, inside and outside her denomination. She was in great demand because she was known to be great to work with, to know the right people to call, and to have a reputation for getting the job done. But now, with each passing week, her to-do list presented an increasing number of tasks left undone, to the point that it seemed almost impossible to make progress.

Feeling totally paralyzed by her overwhelming load, Susan decided she needed a coach. She wasn't sure how she got to this place, and she certainly didn't know what to do to get out of it.

In early coaching sessions Susan talked about how big and impossible her situation was. She had trouble actually brainstorming about options for possible actions to take because it would mean an even longer to-do list. She wasn't really aware that she could not participate in the brainstorming, but her coach noticed.

When her coach asked her to develop a mission, vision, and purpose statement for her life, Susan saw those assignments as just more tasks on her to-do list—more work in her already overwhelming schedule. But out of desperation she did it anyway. Soon she began to use those statements as tools to help her determine when she would say yes to a new assignment and when she would say no.

Her mission, vision, and purpose statements provided the new camera she needed. She learned to say *no*—two small letters, one of the first words children learn. It seemed so simple, but it was a major life event for Susan. Prior to coaching, she unconsciously felt that she was not allowed to say no to anyone. With coaching, she learned that she was the only expert on her own abilities and her vision for her life. Using that little word *no* freed her for even greater productivity. Once again, when her activities were aligned with her mission, her efforts were counting for the Kingdom.

Susan felt so good about this change in her life that she decided to use her coaching sessions to tackle one challenge at a time. In doing that she started making even more progress.

She also noticed that saying no did not bring as many negative consequences as she had originally imagined. In fact, staying focused allowed her to develop a reputation for being an expert in her area of calling, and she started being asked to do things that were much more in line with what she really felt called to do. Clear about how her strengths played into the clarity of her calling, she amazed herself at how much she could accomplish. Instead of being stretched in every direction, she was focused in one direction and felt like she was actually getting somewhere.

A new camera is a good thing!

The Need for Clarity

An out-of-focus camera can still take pictures. So can one with a smudge on the lens or one used in poor lighting or shadows, but you probably won't be very pleased when the photographs are developed. Your pictures probably will not reflect well the image you wanted to capture. If you knew as you took the picture that you would not get the result you seek, you probably just wouldn't bother to take the picture at all.

In life, as in photography, being clear is more important than being beautiful. Even if the picture is not beautiful, if it is clear and focused, you can then start to work on enhancing the picture. Without clarity and focus, you have no hope for enhancement.

Keeping life in focus requires a mental exercise to achieve clarity. Clarity in life involves knowing who you are and what you are called to do. For this you have to know what your strengths are and how those strengths can be used in your calling.

Mental exercises to achieve clarity may also involve seeing patterns and synergies in different aspects of your life. Dr. Jerry Fletcher has developed a way of helping people see the patterns of their high performance.[1] Through his research involving more than six thousand people, he has seen that people have a unique pattern that they follow every time they are functioning at their absolute best.

When I first heard of this, I was a bit skeptical. But when I met Jerry, read his book, and actually worked with him to help find that pattern for myself, it really did contribute to my own clarity about who I am and how I function at my best. The way Jerry describes this is having a "privilege of seeing into the soul of the person to get a glimpse of what God intended when he made you."[2] Now that I have learned to identify my personal pattern, I can also tell when I'm working in or out of that pattern. When I realize I'm not functioning at my peak, I can generally go back to my pattern and find where I'm off. Then I can readjust.

Knowing my pattern of peak performance was a great start but not enough to bring full clarity and focus. My first coach asked me to read a book by Laurie Beth Jones entitled *The Path*.[3] The purpose of that exercise was to help me develop personal mission, vision, and purpose statements. Just reading the book brought clarity and focus to my life, even though, I now admit, I only halfheartedly did the exercises suggested in the book. Years later I asked Laurie Beth to be my coach. She graciously agreed but with the stipulation that I would actually do all the work this time.

What an amazing gift it has been to remain "on the path," having been guided through that process by Laurie Beth! Many clients later,

I'm still suggesting that ministry leaders take a new look at their calling by reading *The Path,* even if in years past they have developed personal mission, vision, and purpose statements. I want them to reconnect with the clarity and focus that comes from that experience. In fact, now that a couple of years have passed since I first read *The Path,* I'm looking again at my mission, vision, and purpose statements. Thank goodness, I'm changing and growing, which means I need to keep getting new cameras.

Having a mission statement is not enough; you have to *live* it. Since your soul is that part of you that connects you to God and persists for eternity, living life oriented around the purpose that God created you for is part of "loving the Lord with all of your soul" as well.

A Single Focus

The key to clarity is simplicity. It is much more difficult to find clarity in the midst of complexity. All of us live complex lives today. Many things distract us from seeing what is most important. With so much clutter in our lives, sometimes it is difficult to see what is essential and meaningful. A *Christ-Centered* coach can help at this point.

Benefits of Coaching

Coaching Others		God-Sized Goals
Intentional Progress		
Clarity/Focus	Confidence	Learning
Orienting around Strengths		

Finding our focus points to action. Just as the purpose of finding focus with a camera is to take a picture, the purpose of finding focus in our lives is to take constructive action in our lives. Taking the right actions, actions that make us feel productive and let us know we are fulfilling our God-given purpose, is dependent on having clarity–clarity of mission, vision, purpose; clarity about our God-given strengths and what we are best suited to do in the Kingdom.

Sometimes we may have moments when we feel we are connected with our work, our ministry, and with those around us. But that clarity can be fleeting, especially if we have not identified our own essential best patterns of working. Diligence is needed to gain this type of clarity and to stay focused.

Often when we are not clear about our best patterns of working, we fail to choose–not just fail to choose what's best; we fail to choose at all. Like Susan, we don't know the meaning of the word *no.* But what we fail to realize is that not choosing is a choice in itself.

Keeping life in focus is a conscious act of alignment—aligning actions, thoughts, attitudes, and language to be congruent with the clarity gained around calling and strengths. Achieving and maintaining focus involves getting specific about what you will do—and will not do; what you will do today as well as what you will do a year from now, determining priorities for both the long term and the short term. Staying in focus, then, means developing communication strategies to help you as you relate to others so that they will begin to understand that your focus determines what you will and won't do. Good communication will clarify for others that, by eliminating the things that are not a fit or that would get you distracted, you can be even more productive in doing what God has called and equipped you to do. Often the process will greatly narrow the scope of your activities and simplify your life even more.

Clarity and Focus—the Essential Combination

The words *clarity* and *focus* are similar and almost interchangeable, yet distinction is helpful to identify steps for the person to take to achieve and maintain self-understanding, to find a clear vision, and to be able to take the steps necessary to follow it. It's no accident that *vision*—a word used to capture a person's dreams, aspirations, purpose, mission, and call—requires the ability to see into the future. Without clarity and focus, a clean camera lens for the soul, most people can't see what needs to be done today, much less into the future. Acts are random instead of channeled. Answering yes to any and every task stirs up a subconscious hope that by trying many things we will accidentally stumble on the one that somehow brings satisfaction.

Finding clarity and focus doesn't come through random events. It doesn't usually come with a single "aha" moment. In reality, clarity may only come one step at a time. Remember what the psalmist said? "Your word is a lamp to my feet / and a light to my path" (Psalm 119:105). Light for the path comes just one step at a time. While we can take steps to find clarity and focus, working with purpose and vision is also an act of faith.

Whom do you know who seems to have clarity and focus? How will you recognize such a person? Someone with clarity and focus uses language like this:

"I know what to do but not how to do it."
"That is not something I need to do; that can be done by someone else."

"I'm confident about my calling. I'm just trying to determine my options within my field of opportunities."

On the other hand, someone lacking clarity and focus uses language like this:

"I'm not sure."
"Things look fuzzy to me."
"I'm so confused."

You know the old phrase: "jack of all trades, master of none"? That can easily apply to someone without focus and clarity. We learned in our last chapter that each of us has mastered skills apart from our strength base. We are all capable of doing many things well. But not everything is a good fit for our strengths and our best way of doing things.

It is easy for ministerial professionals to slip into such a role. It seems to go along with the servant model, thinking you have to say yes to every request, whether you have time, inclination, or aptitude. Not everything we don't like about a job can be eliminated, of course; but many things can be delegated to people who have the gifts, strengths, and skills to do them. To be a minister really doesn't mean you have to say yes to everything.

Inhibitors to Clarity and Focus

The relationship of "clarity and focus" to "strengths" is clear. It's difficult to talk about clarity and focus without referring to strengths and skills. That's why clarity and focus form the next building block in *Christ-Centered* coaching benefits. Clarity and focus are generally the next step in progression of a coaching relationship.

In a coaching relationship, you will likely identify in your life some common inhibitors to clarity and focus. Finding and eliminating those inhibitors will be like cleaning the lens of the camera. Getting rid of the inhibitors is essential to achieving clarity and focus. Among the inhibitors you are likely to discover are these.

Getting value from false sources

Everyone likes to feel needed and important. Sometimes we struggle with the need for affirmation. When what we are doing does not give us that self-satisfaction, we turn to others for validation. When people come to us and ask us to do anything, we feel affirmed, needed, important.

The good feeling of being needed is often overpowered by the negative feeling of doing things you don't want to do or don't have time to do or have no interest in doing. With clarity and focus, you will find that true value comes from being who you were created to be.

Not being able to say no

Clarity and focus require discipline and the willingness not to do some things. Paul says it well in 1 Corinthians 9:24–27:

> Do you not know that in a race the runners all compete, but only one receives the prize? Run in such a way that you may win it. Athletes exercise self-control in all things; they do it to receive a perishable wreath, but we an imperishable one. So I do not run aimlessly, nor do I box as though beating the air; but I punish my body and enslave it, so that after proclaiming to others I myself should not be disqualified.

Paul was always focused on preaching the good news of the resurrected Lord. The images of running aimlessly or boxing at air are perfect metaphors for lack of focus. And the discipline of training the body is a good metaphor for one who has clarity and focus. Achieving this level of benefit from *Christ-Centered* coaching doesn't come the first week. It takes work, discipline.

Letting the job control identity and calendar

Often people have this backward; they let the organization or their current job description dictate their actions. They think they have to do everything they are asked to do to achieve success, to reach the next level, to be highly regarded by peers and management.

Such was Susan's situation. But if you do that for too long, you will start to feel trapped. You *do* have a choice. Another way to operate is to see your current position as one part of your lifelong ministry.

Having too little time

People don't plan, because they say planning takes time, yet all planners know that planning saves many hours somewhere along the line. The same is true with achieving clarity and focus. It gets back to simplicity. Our overly complex lives often result from a lack of clarity and focus.

A lack of clarity and focus actually wastes time in doing tasks that are not a good fit and in being unproductive in those mismatched jobs. Finding clarity and focus may take a little time in the present, but the benefits quickly accrue. Like money saved when young, the dividends continue to grow over a lifetime.

Seeming importance of comparison to others

Calling is unique for each individual, yet it is only human to compare our efforts with those of others to see if we are doing well, to see if we are succeeding. Instead of using external criteria by comparing ourselves to others to measure success, a better assessment is to look inward to see where we are in accomplishing what God has called us to do.

Moses, Aaron, David, Peter, Paul are heroes of the faith. Each had a distinct calling, but none of these men could have done well what the others did.

The Role of the *Christ-Centered* Coach in Achieving Clarity and Focus

By the time you are ready to work on your clarity and focus, your coach will know you well and will have determined specific strategies to help you reach this next level of benefits. You can expect to hear your coach ask questions like these:

- What is your mission, vision, purpose? *(clarity)*
- What are your short-term and long-term goals? *(clarity)*
- What is your role in accomplishing them, and who else is needed to accomplish them? *(clarity)*
- What long-term and short-term results do you anticipate? *(clarity)*
- How can you narrow the scope of your current job? *(focus)*
- What one thing is most important to tackle today? *(focus)*
- What would be the easiest three things for you to complete this week? *(focus)*
- What can you do that would make the largest or most immediate impact for the people you serve? *(focus)*
- What can you say no to, that you'd really rather not do, to say yes to something you'd love to do? *(focus)*
- What can you stop doing to make room for something new and more important or more impactful? *(focus)*
- How can you say no to the requester and still satisfy your goals and theirs? *(focus)*
- Who can you champion/develop/sponsor/recommend to do the things that you are clear are no longer things you can do and stay focused? *(focus)*
- How can you make your actions match your words on the topic of priorities? *(focus)*
- Where do you spend the most time? Is that what is most important in your list of priorities? If not, how can the amount of time you spend more closely reflect the importance? *(focus)*

- Where do you spend the most money/budget? Is that the most impactful use of those resources? If not, how can you align the expenses with the return? *(focus)*

You can attempt to find clarity and focus on your own, of course, without a coach. The challenge is that we often don't hold ourselves accountable. We often break promises to ourselves when we won't break a promise to someone else. Since finding clarity and focus is a discipline—like living a healthy lifestyle by eating the right food, getting enough sleep, exercising—it is easy to put ourselves last, others first, and not fulfill promises to ourselves. Working with a *Christ-Centered* coach, making a commitment to another person, knowing we will talk with that person about that commitment soon moves us to live more disciplined lives. We'll talk about this in greater depth in the next chapter.

Another difficulty with attempting to find clarity and focus on your own is that you have to adopt a different perspective to see a whole, clear picture. As with the camera, you cannot tell how the picture will look when you are in the picture, but the person looking through the lens of the camera has a much better idea of how the picture will turn out. Sometimes you need to step out of the picture and behind the lens of the camera to get the clarity and focus you need. A *Christ-Centered* coach can help you do that. A coach can encourage you to step behind the camera. A coach can give you an honest appraisal of the image seen through his or her lens, an objective appraisal of you as the subject of the picture. A coach's viewpoint can give a very different perspective from the one you see as a subject of the picture.

Achieving clarity and focus is a constant activity, not a one-time event resolved for a lifetime. It's a concept consistent with biblical teaching. We are constantly being made new, receiving new mercies every day.

Look at your photo album. Instead of one picture, your life is a series of pictures in which the environment you find yourself in is constantly changing. Look at the photos of yourself. They're taken at different times and in different places to reflect different points, interests, and activities in your life. Take a closer look. You don't look the same in every picture. You grow and change over time. When you look at those photos, you probably recall times in your life that make you smile. Others may be less pleasing. Where did those wrinkles come from? When did I gain that ten pounds? Time passes before you know it, and changes occur without our paying attention.

It's the same with clarity and focus. Time can lull you into thinking that the clarity and focus you had right out of seminary will still serve you five, ten, or even twenty-five years later. But you've learned much in experience and in other ways since seminary. Your lens on life needs to adjust, too. Your worldview, while based on the same principles, will adjust to your growth, to your environment, and to your ability to express it. Instead of constancy and lack of change, clarity and focus actually help us in the process of reinvention, in our ability to react in our world in ways that adjust our calling, vision, purpose to what God is doing in the world and is calling us to join him in doing.

Isn't this consistent with what the Bible says? Becoming a Christian and then growing as a disciple are all about change.

> So if anyone is in Christ, there is a new creation: everything old has passed away; see, everything has become new! (2 Corinthians 5:17)

> Create in me a clean heart, O God,
>   and put a new and right spirit within me. (Psalm 51:10)

> Jesus answered him, "Very truly, I tell you, no one can see the kingdom of God without being born from above." (John 3:3)

> "Truly I tell you, unless you change and become like children, you will never enter the kingdom of heaven. Whoever becomes humble like this child is the greatest in the kingdom of heaven." (Matthew 18:3–4)

> But when the goodness and loving kindness of God our Savior appeared, he saved us, not because of any works of righteousness that we had done, but according to his mercy, through the water of rebirth and renewal by the Holy Spirit. This Spirit he poured out on us richly through Jesus Christ our Savior, so that, having been justified by his grace, we might become heirs according to the hope of eternal life. The saying is sure. (Titus 3:4–8a)

When you are actively pursuing clarity and focus, you'll find that you have no capacity or energy for politics (a distraction). More of your efforts will go toward your calling.

When you are actively pursuing clarity and focus, the results of that discipline start to permeate your life. I have had clients decide to make family time a priority and leave their briefcase with laptop in the car at night, begin dancing lessons with a spouse to prioritize that relationship, schedule time on the playground with children on a weeknight, schedule their part-time work on only certain days of the week so that the other days are available to be spent with grandchildren, or ride bikes on the weekend to favorite picnic spots. In each of these cases, the person being coached did not intend to deal with family issues during our calls, but clarity and focus actually spilled over into all aspects of their life.

When you are actively pursuing clarity and focus, the picture gets bigger, not smaller. You might think that saying no and eliminating distractions is a way of making the scope smaller, but actually, when you gain clarity and focus, you can step up to having a greater impact in the areas of your strength than you ever could without clarity and focus.[4]

Loving the Lord with all your strength means not only knowing what your strengths are but also having the clarity and focus to use those strengths in the context of your calling—constantly, consistently, even when the world is changing all around you.

The decision to pursue clarity and focus requires making a shift in thinking about who you are and aligning your actions with the priorities you determine in the process. Jesus refers to this in Luke 19:46. He's quoting from Jeremiah 7:1–11, which says (among other things):

1. acknowledge God's sovereignty,
2. change your thinking, and
3. adjust your action.

In Luke 19:46, Jesus was angered because, once again, these steps were not happening (apologies to the pastor, whom I cannot recall, who shared this Scripture and insight with me).

A Life Brought into Focus

At the heart of effective coaching is a shift in thinking on the part of the client that results in realigning actions with the new thinking. Coaching skills, competencies, and models center around facilitating that process of shifting and moving forward.

Let me tell you a story about a corporate client, not a minister.[5] His poignant story is about the power of this concept of shifting. This executive client, who had experienced this shifting as a result of months of coaching sessions, said one day, "Jane, I finally get it!"

At that point I started rewinding the tape in my mind as fast as I could to remember what in the world it was that he didn't get last time that we talked so that I could anticipate what he now felt he understood.

He couldn't have surprised me more by saying, "I finally get it. Being 'born again' is just a shift, right?"

Oh, my! What a statement! Here was one of those rare points in my life where I was almost speechless.

The surprise was that he and I had *never* talked about being "born again." In fact, I don't even recall that we had ever talked about values and beliefs and their role in decision making. So I pulled it together and stayed in the role of coach as much as possible. I followed his statement with, "Yes, I believe you are right. Being 'born again' is just a shift." Then I asked, "What brought this up? I don't remember talking about this before."

He said, "I had heard someone talk about this before, and I had heard that you are a Christian. When I heard the term 'born again' before, I thought it sounded crazy, but now that I've been being coached for a while, it dawned on me that that concept was really about making a shift in thinking and realigning your actions with that new thinking—just like you've taught me in coaching sessions."

He had experienced success through the really hard work of changing his mind, aligning actions with new thinking, dealing with employees who didn't understand his shift at first, and then seeing the positive results of those changes.

I continued, "What do you want to do with this new awareness you have gained?"

"I think I want to make a shift in my thinking to believe in Jesus."

After a big gulp, I pressed on: "OK, what next?"

"I guess I need to realign my actions to that shift."

Be still, my heart. "OK, what actions would you like to take?"

"I'm not really sure what the appropriate actions are that align with believing Jesus. That's where I'm stuck."

Note to self: keep coaching. "Where do you think you could learn about this?"

"Maybe the Bible would be a place to start."

"OK. So tell me specifically, what action are you going to take?

"I'm going to read the Bible."

"It's a really long book. How long do you think it will take you?"

"I'm not sure. I've never read it before. I don't even have one. I'll get one and just start at the beginning, like I would any book and see where that takes me."

At this point I couldn't stand it anymore. I try so hard not to suggest actions for my clients and allow them to design their actions themselves. That's generally the best plan. However, in this case, I decided to ask permission to partner with him in the design of the action. So I said, "Can I make a suggestion? If you want to learn about Jesus, how about starting with the Book of John? It's not at the beginning of the Bible, but you don't have to have read all the parts prior to it to understand it. Really, the Bible is an anthology of several books that can be read independently. I'm suggesting the Book of John because it talks a lot about the purpose of Jesus' life and that is where you will find the phrase 'born again.'"

"OK, sure. I'll read the Book of John."

Such conversations are among the most amazing *Christ-Centered* coaching experiences of my life. All ministry leaders need those high affirmation days. As a missionary to the workplace, I include myself in that description.

As ministry leaders, including myself again, we need to be the best models of shifting on the planet. If we can do it, we can lead others through it.

Focusing on Scripture

God promises to care for you and expects focus in return:

The LORD is my shepherd, I shall not want.
He makes me lie down in green pastures;
he leads me beside still waters;
he restores my soul.
He leads me in the right paths
for his name's sake. (Psalm 23:1–3)

God promises light, one step at a time:

Your word is a lamp to my feet
and a light to my path. (Psalm 119:105)

You are transformed by the renewing of your mind, and you can know God's will for your life:

Do not be conformed to this world, but be transformed by the renewing of your minds, so that you may discern what is the will of God—what is good and acceptable and perfect. (Romans 12:2)

God gives new mercies each day:

The steadfast love of the LORD never ceases,
his mercies never come to an end;
they are new every morning;
great is your faithfulness. (Lamentations 3:22–23)

To keep focused on the race you are to run, you can allow no distractions:

> Therefore, since we are surrounded by so great a cloud of witnesses, let us also lay aside every weight and the sin that clings to closely, and let us run with perseverance the race that is set before us, looking to Jesus the pioneer and perfecter of our faith, who for the sake of the joy that was set before him endured the cross, disregarding its shame, and has taken his seat at the right hand of the throne of God.
>
> Consider him who endured such hostility against himself from sinners, so that you may not grow weary or lose heart. (Hebrews 12:1–3)

You need to have discipline to compete in the race:

> Do you not know that in a race the runners all compete, but only one receives the prize? Run in such a way that you may win it. Athletes exercise self-control in all things; they do it to receive a perishable wreath, but we an imperishable one. So I do not run aimlessly, nor do I box as though beating the air; but I punish my body and enslave it, so that after proclaiming to others I myself should not be disqualified. (1 Corinthians 9:24–27)

Tips for *Christ-Centered* Coaches

- A great question for beginning down the path to clarity and focus is, "Where are you, and where do you want to be?" For Christians, "Where does God want you to be?"
- Don't be surprised if clients can't answer either of those questions at first. After all, if they could answer them easily, they probably wouldn't be stuck in the first place.

Tips for Working with a *Christ-Centered* Coach

- If you haven't written mission, vision, and purpose statements, do it now. They will give you a new camera for your life.
- Even if you have written mission, vision, and purpose statements for your life before, do it again; life changes. Update them now and then.
- Practice saying no. You might try listing all the positives that will come from saying no and engage an objective observer in helping you develop this list prior to practicing saying no. Begin by saying no to little things, and build up to saying no to everything that doesn't fit your mission.

CHAPTER 6

Christ-Centered Coaching
Instills Confidence

*I hereby command you: Be strong and courageous; do not be frightened
or dismayed, for the LORD your God is with you wherever you go.*

JOSHUA 1:9

Fred already had everything he needed to succeed. He had a
solid educational background. He had served supportive churches
that nurtured him as a young pastor. He had workable, creative ideas.
And he had an enviable family situation with a loving wife who
respected him.

So what was his problem? Why was he stuck? Why wasn't he
moving forward?

Things were changing. Fred felt as if he were caught in a whirl-
wind. His world seemed to be changing ever faster, and the changes
were consistently more drastic, even frightening.

Fred had read about coaching for pastors in a national magazine
for ministry leaders. From what he'd read, he thought that maybe a
coach could help him get a handle on all the change happening in
his life.

In one of his early coaching sessions, Fred used a visual image to
describe his ministry as looking like one of those little battery-operated
cars that bump into things and then back up, turn, and find something

else to bump into. In fact, in his scenario, the walls kept moving in closer and closer so that he was bumping into things more and more often.

Then his coach asked, "What are the walls that are preventing your forward movement?"

"I have what I think are some good ideas, but I'm not sure they'll work."

"What's stopping you from trying?"

"Nothing, really. I just don't know if the changes I envision will move the church in the right direction. The changes will cost a lot of money; and if the plan doesn't work, the money will have been wasted."

"Is that all that's stopping you?"

"No, it's not that simple. If I waste the money, the people in my church will think less of me. One of my friends tried something new in his church, nothing like this idea, but he tried something that wasted money, and he is not at that church anymore...I don't really have proof that this will work. Maybe I should wait until I get more information. I'm thinking better about this now."

After a long pause the coach asked, "Fred, what are you really afraid of?"

That was it. Fred stopped in his tracks. He felt like he might suffocate because that was such a poignant word—*afraid.* He didn't really consider himself as someone who was fearful, but that really was it. A better question would have been, "What are you not afraid of?" because it would have had a shorter answer.

Fred was afraid of wasting money. He was afraid of what others would think of him. He was afraid of not being able to succeed at any other line of work if his reputation was ruined by making a big mistake. He was afraid of losing the respect of his wife and children. His list of fears went on and on. At the heart of it, he was afraid of failure or, worse, being discovered as a fraud.

Fred wasn't a fraud. But things had been changing so fast that he had to think on his feet a lot and constantly wondered if he really knew what he was doing anymore.

The topic of the next several coaching sessions was fear. First, Fred had to let go of having to be perfect. He also had to adopt action strategies for addressing his fears versus avoiding them. In the process, Fred realized that much of what he feared was not grounded in reality but had been exaggerated by his lack of confidence in dealing with change.

Over time Fred transitioned from thinking of his life as an out-of-control bumper car to that of a high-performance race car engineered for making forward progress with a fearless driver.

Fears and Frauds

People being coached commonly need confidence. One benefit of *Christ-Centered* coaching is developing greater confidence in your ability to come up with good ideas and to carry them out. The problem is not that ministry leaders are timid or weak. Ministry leaders must deal with hidden fears on an almost daily basis. To compensate for a lack of confidence, sometimes ministry leaders develop a false veneer of self-confidence. On the outside it looks like they are the epitome of confidence; on the inside that could not be further from the truth.

Benefits of Coaching

Coaching Others		God-Sized Goals	
Intentional Progress			
Clarity/Focus	**Confidence**		Learning
Orienting around Strengths			

Christ-Centered coaches can help ministers discover and develop tools to address their fears. By talking through your fears with a coach—an environment in which you can be open and honest—you can unashamedly express your fears to someone who will allow you to be a different person each day. That doesn't mean you're wishy-washy or inconsistent; rather, the coaching relationship allows you to make mental shifts, to think different thoughts, to express aloud what you are thinking without the fear of being laughed at, judged, or being told you're crazy.

Eventually, the freedom to make mental shifts in a safe environment will lead to action. A coach can help you develop customized actions grounded in wisdom for each fear. Remember that James wrote, "If any of you is lacking in wisdom, ask God, who gives to all generously and ungrudgingly, and it will be given you" (James 1:5).

A *Christ-Centered* coaching relationship is a safe place, an absolutely confidential relationship where you can try out ideas and fail. The coach will still be there unconditionally to support you in picking yourself up and trying again.

Everyone needs a safe place to:

1. *Discover*–If you discover something new as a result of a coaching session, it has to be OK that you didn't know it before. Pride has to go. An external sign that coaching is needed in this area is that you are not making any progress and that you are not making any effort to get help in moving ahead. Such behavior may be the result of fear. Moving past that can help you discover many new things about yourself and your environment. These new discoveries may be just the thing to start the momentum moving in a positive direction.

2. *Create*–The creative process is not a smooth one. Some people have to talk to create; others have to spend a lot of time thinking. In either case a coaching conversation is a great place to try out ideas on an objective third party. If you need to try out a tough conversation—perhaps one that just thinking about creates anxiety—you can role-play with your coach to "create" the messages you really want to get across. Such role play can allow you to test your words, your tone, and the clarity of the message. This is just one example of a creative idea you might test with a coach.

3. *Transform*–Only a few relationships are open to ongoing growth and change. Many relationships don't allow you to be different tomorrow from the way you were yesterday. But that has to happen to make forward progress. In fact, Paul wrote it as a command,

> Do not be conformed to this world, but be transformed by the renewing of your minds, so that you may discern what is the will of God—what is good and acceptable and perfect. (Romans 12:2)

Not only will a *Christ-Centered* coach allow you to grow and change; a coach will expect it.

Imagine what it would be like to begin every day of your ministry with *confidence:*

- the kind of confidence that allows you the leeway to discover applications for ministry that you have never seen before,
- the kind of confidence that provides inspiration and safety to create new ways of doing ministry that could have greater impact than before,
- the kind of confidence that yields freedom to leave behind your old behaviors in favor of all the new and improved ones that you feel led to adopt.

What would your ministry look like then? Since we are dreaming, let's keep going. Imagine what it would be like if every ministry leader that you work with had the same type of confidence. The congregations, denominations, and organizations that you are part of would have formidable impact! With coaching this is not a pipe dream; it is a possibility. I have the privileged front-row seat to see it happen frequently.

The Role of the *Christ-Centered* Coach

How does a *Christ-Centered* coaching relationship actually instill confidence?

A *Christ-Centered* coach offers encouragement. That doesn't mean you can expect to receive false praise from your coach, but it does mean that a coach will affirm your strengths. A coach will offer true encouragement like the writer of Hebrews had in mind: "But exhort [*NIV*, "encourage"] one another every day, as long as it is called 'today,' so that none of you may be hardened by the deceitfulness of sin" (Hebrews 3:13). It is encouragement fueled by adversity, the kind Paul wrote about: "Most of the brothers and sisters, having been made confident in the Lord by my imprisonment, dare to speak the word with greater boldness and without fear" (Philippians 1:14). It is encouragement to a ministry leader so that in all ways you might exalt Jesus Christ. Again, Paul wrote, "It is my eager expectation and hope that I will not be put to shame in any way, but that by my speaking with all boldness, Christ will be exalted now as always in my body, whether by life or by death" (Philippians 1:20).

- A *Christ-Centered* coach will challenge you to reach your full Kingdom potential.
- A *Christ-Centered* coach will believe in you when you don't even believe in yourself.
- A *Christ-Centered* coach provides feedback as if holding up a mirror so that you can take an honest look at yourself and your situation.

Ministry leaders often feel that they are expected to have all the answers. They learn to act with confidence whether they feel confident or not. Sometimes when they know they are *acting* confident, they begin to feel like frauds. You are not a fraud. You just might need some encouragement and a safe place to experiment with new ideas to build confidence.

Recently I asked about twenty-five ministry leaders who had benefited from coaching to give me the highlights of those benefits. I thought they might mention getting clarity or knowing more about their strengths. But the most frequently mentioned benefits were related to this topic of confidence. Respondents worded their benefits in different ways, but they pointed to the same area—confidence. The confidence benefits they listed were:

- "Having a thought partner."
- "Having a sounding board, a chance to hear myself voice new ideas and to work through the kinks in a conversation instead of trying the half-baked idea out on others before getting a chance to refine it."
- "Having a nonjudgmental person to reflect with me. Having a person listen to my opinions without judging me as a person as I expressed new ideas." (Coaches are trained to know how to do this, but random coworkers and laypeople may not be.)

The Need for Confidence

What does lack of confidence look like?

- Hesitancy, second guessing
- Satisfaction with the status quo
- Analysis paralysis
- Excessive comparisons to others
- Neediness
- Bumper cars!

What does confidence look like?

- Constant experimentation
- Implementation of plans, noting ways to improve, adjusting, reimplementing
- Attracting others to join you
- A race car!

Perhaps one of your favorite Bible personalities alternated between having confidence and lack of confidence:

- Moses showed courage when he spoke to Pharaoh, but earlier he told God that he couldn't speak. He needed Aaron to speak for him.
- Gideon kept asking God to tell him one more time what he wanted him to do, but he showed bravery in battle.
- Peter denied knowing Jesus and hid out with the other disciples after the crucifixion. But he also demonstrated the faith on which Jesus would build his church, and he confidently served until his

death, whether preaching with power at Pentecost, or imprisoned in a jail cell.

What would even a little more confidence do for you?

- Free you from paralyzing fear.
- Help you assess risks more accurately and put possible results to your actions in more realistic perspective.
- Enable you to have a tough conversation with a person in your church that you have been avoiding.
- Provide you with the opportunity to try new things and learn from your mistakes.
- Begin your collection of small successes that can be put together to create even greater success.
- Establish a knowledge base of what works and what doesn't that will be the foundation of data needed to make even more successful plans in the future.
- Help you pull things together after something doesn't work out so that you can try again.
- Inspire others to try new things after watching the example of your fearlessness.
- Foster your exploration of new territories.
- Head you in the direction of tackling something so big that you cannot even imagine being able to do it without God's help (see chapter 10, "*Christ-Centered* Coaching Encourages God-sized Goals").

A Story of Confidence

Here's a *Christ-Centered* coaching illustration that has a direct relationship to ministry. It is about the combined benefits of clarity/ focus and confidence. It is also about using coaching as a parenting tool. Unlike the rest of the stories in this book, this one recounts a specific session with a specific person—my son, Andrew. Not only do I have Andrew's permission to tell you this story, but he also helped me remember some of the parts that I had forgotten.

We all know that teenagers often resist being "told." I know I did when I was that age. I guess I still do, in fact. Our sons are no different from other teenagers. We try to coach them as often as the situation allows and find that we get better results when we can remember to coach instead of instruct.

When our son, Andrew, was sixteen, he was the youth representative on a selection committee to find a new youth pastor for our church. He was honored to be asked to be on the committee and also a little intimidated to be the only teenager in so many meetings with all adults.

Early in the process the committee decided on the formal process for selecting a youth pastor. They determined how they would share that information with the church and also get input on the characteristics people wanted in a new youth pastor. The plan was to have two communication meetings concurrently, one with the parents and one with the youth (about eighty kids). Andrew would be responsible for the presentation to the youth. Most of the adults on the committee would share the responsibility for running the meeting with the parents, and he had the main responsibility for running the meeting with the youth, with some support from a couple of the adult committee members.

He was pretty nervous because this was the first time he had ever done anything like this. It was important to him to do a good job not only because he wanted his friends to be pleased but also because he realized it was a big deal to find the person that God wanted for the job. His presentation was to take place on a Sunday evening, so that Sunday after lunch he came and asked me if we could have a coaching session. At that point I didn't know what the topic was.

I said, "OK, I'm not going to be mom in this conversation, so don't try to second-guess what I want your answers to be. I'm going to be a coach, and when I ask a question, I really don't know the answer. I'm trying to get you to use what *you know* to figure out a solution. Deal?"

"Deal."

"What's up?"

"I've got to present the process for selecting a youth pastor to the youth group tonight. I feel a little unprepared because this is a big undertaking. Everything I've experienced on the committee so far has been taking in information, and tonight is all about putting it out there correctly for my peers."

"Let's take it one step at a time. What do you need to do?"

"I need to figure out what to say tonight at the youth group meeting about how the selection process will work."

"Is that all?"

"And I need to ask them to fill out a survey to find out what they want us to look for in a youth pastor."

"Anything else?"

"I think that's it."

"OK, what do they need to understand?"

"The kids need to know why we are a committee and what we are going to be doing."

"How can you do that?"

"I don't know! If I knew that, I wouldn't have to come to you, Mom."

"Tell me what you *do* know, and we'll go from there."

Andrew explained the answers to both of those questions–why they are a committee and what they would be doing. He said they had put the process into a set of steps.

"What are the steps?"

Andrew described an elaborate twelve-step process that the committee would go through in choosing a youth pastor. He demonstrated to me that he really understood the steps, because he could rattle them off so quickly. That's when I figured out that the problem was not that he didn't understand; it was that he didn't know how to organize the information to present it.

"How could you convey this in a way that the youth group could really get it?"

"I think it is too much for me to read to them; that would sound really boring. I know that I will give them a handout with information on it that we developed in the committee, but this process is going to take months, so the chances of them keeping up with a handout for that long are not so good."

"How else could you convey this process to them?"

"If they had some kind of visual for the annex (the youth gathering room) to keep up with the progress, that would probably be the best thing."

"What could that look like?"

"I guess I could make a poster."

"Would that achieve all of what you want to accomplish?"

"I'd need some way to keep updating them on where we are in the process."

"How could you do that?"

"I have an idea. I could make a little arrow that has double-stick tape on the back and then just move the arrow to the next step when we make progress."

"That's a great idea. Do you have everything you need to make your poster?"

"Yep."

"Well then, sounds like a plan."

That was actually part one of about three parts to an afternoon of coaching sessions. Before the day was over, we had also coached around determining the key messages that were not on the poster, how he would explain them, and the order he would follow. By the time that he left for church that night, he was really ready. He was still a little nervous, but he left with more confidence that he knew what he was doing.

We went to the parents' meeting, so we didn't get to see the result of the coaching session; but we heard about it later. People said, "Wow, Andrew really did a nice job at that meeting."

He came back home that night bubbling over to tell us how well it went and feeling confident that he had done the best he could. The poster stayed in the annex for months, and Andrew kept everyone informed by just moving the arrow. Parents told me they stopped by to see the arrow instead of asking a committee member for an update.

This story illustrates a couple of benefits of coaching. When you ask Andrew what the benefit of coaching is, he says, "It helps me get my thoughts organized and feel good enough to get out there and try something I've never done before."

Don't we all need that?

"And a little child will lead them"–and we're privileged when ours does the leading.

Confidence in God's Word

One way to have confidence is to instill it in others:

> I thank my God every time I remember you, constantly praying with joy in every one of my prayers for all of you, because of your sharing in the gospel from the first day until now. I am confident of this, that the one who began a good work among you will bring it to completion by the day of Jesus Christ. (Philippians 1:3–6)

You can also build confidence in others by wanting more for others than they want for themselves:

> And this is my prayer, that your love may overflow more and more with knowledge and full insight to help you determine what is best, so that in the day of Christ you may be pure and blameless, having produced the harvest of righteousness that comes through Jesus Christ for the glory and praise of God. (Philippians 1:9–11)

Knowing God provides a safe place in every storm:

> One day he got into a boat with his disciples, and he said to them, "Let us go across to the other side of the lake." So they put out, and while they were sailing he fell asleep. A windstorm swept down on the lake, and the boat was filling with water,

and they were in danger. They went to him and woke him up, shouting, "Master, Master, we are perishing!" And he woke up and rebuked the wind and the raging waves; they ceased, and there was a calm. He said to them, "Where is your faith?" They were afraid and amazed, and said to one another, "Who then is this, that he commands even the winds and the water, and they obey him?" (Luke 8:22–25)

Jesus promised not to forsake you. You can have confidence in his promise:

"I will ask the Father, and he will give you another Advocate, to be with you forever." (John 14:16)

Jesus is preparing a place for you:

"Do not let your hearts be troubled. Believe in God, believe also in me...If I go and prepare a place for you, I will come again and will take you to myself, so that where I am, there you may be also." (John 14:1, 3)

Jesus, the living Word, gives power to those who believe:

To all who received him, who believed in his name, he gave power to become children of God. (John 1:12)

With your newfound confidence, you can encourage others:

Judas and Silas, who were themselves prophets, said much to encourage and strengthen the believers. (Acts 15:32)

Our confidence is our ultimate hope in God's promise of eternity with him:

But we do not want you to be uninformed, brothers and sisters, about those who have died, so that you may not grieve as others do who have no hope. For since we believe that Jesus died and rose again, even so, through Jesus, God will bring with him those who have died. For this we declare to you by the word of the Lord, that we who are alive, who are left until the coming of the Lord, will by no means precede those who have died. For the Lord himself, with a cry of command, with the archangel's call and with the sound of God's trumpet, will descend from heaven, and the dead in Christ will rise first. Then we who are alive, who are left, will be caught up in the clouds together with them to meet the Lord in the air; and so we will be with the Lord forever.

Therefore encourage one another with these words.
(1 Thessalonians 4:13–18)

Such words of encouragement helped early believers face persecution and even death because of their confidence in the power and promise of the resurrection.

Ever disciplined, Paul also wrote an antidote for lack of hope:

Proclaim the message; be persistent whether the time is favorable or unfavorable; convince, rebuke, and encourage, with the utmost patience in teaching. (2 Timothy 4:2)

Holding on to such hope and confidence is not optional for ministry leaders—both to give to others and to hold onto for yourself as well.

You can also encourage your fellow ministry leaders and find encouragement in them:

Not neglecting to meet together, as is the habit of some, but encouraging one another, and all the more as you see the Day approaching. (Hebrews 10:25)

We need one another, connected to hope.

John reminds us that the ultimate source of confidence and destroyer of fear is God's love:

By this we know that we abide in him and he in us, because he has given us of his Spirit. And we have seen and do testify that the Father has sent his Son as the Savior of the world. God abides in those who confess that Jesus is the Son of God, and they abide in God. So we have known and believe the love that God has for us.

God is love, and those who abide in love abide in God, and God abides in them. Love has been perfected among us in this: that we may have boldness on the day of judgment, because as he is, so are we in this world. There is no fear in love, but perfect love casts out fear; for fear has to do with punishment, and whoever fears has not reached perfection in love. We love because he first loved us. Those who say, "I love God," and hate their brothers or sisters, are liars; for those who do not love a brother or sister whom they have seen, cannot love God whom they have not seen. The commandment we have from him is this: those who love God must love their bothers and sisters also. (1 John 4:13–21)

As John states here, we love because God first loved us. This benefit is even greater when coaching non-Christians who are not familiar with the type of love available though Jesus Christ. I can tell that some of my corporate clients are often experiencing unconditional love for the first time ever, and they are attracted to it. Because of their lack of exposure to such love and acceptance prior to the *Christ-Centered* coaching relationship, sometimes they connect the term *coaching* to the sensation that was new to them—God's love.

Tips for *Christ-Centered* Coaches

- Work at developing the trust of the ministry leader that you are coaching. He or she has to trust you for your encouragement to have an impact.
- Don't step over fears. If you do, they will too.
- Be careful to use *and* instead of *but.* Everything after the *but* actually negates the encouragement. Remember Job's friends? "Your words have supported those who were stumbling, / and you have made firm the feeble knees. / But now it has come to you, and you are impatient; / it touches you, and you are dismayed" (Job 4:4–5). Job's friends are actually good examples of how to *discourage.*
- Be specific in your encouragement. Generalizations sound canned and come across as disingenuous.
- Study Paul. He was a great encourager.
- If you want to learn how to help instill courage, check out what Scripture says about loving one another. This would be the part of the Great Commandment that says "and love your neighbor as yourself."

Tips for Working with a *Christ-Centered* Coach

- Work on developing trust with your coach so that you can address fears. Be open early in the relationship even when it might feel uncomfortable.
- Say good-bye to the lie that perfection is possible. If you'll go ahead and do that, you can make progress quicker.
- Trust the encouragement of your coach. If your coach believes in a dream for you, don't dismiss it out of hand. Several of my coaches have believed in me long before I could believe in myself. I'm convinced that being open to trusting their opinions of my abilities and me helped me achieve the dreams they believed on my behalf before I did.

CHAPTER 7

Christ-Centered Coaching Catapults Learning

*Let the wise also hear and gain in learning,
and the discerning acquire skill.*

PROVERBS 1:5

Rachel is a new pastor at an innovative church; some would call it an emerging church. Rachel had worked with a coach for over six months prior to moving to this church. In fact, the plan to transition to this church had come from some of her early sessions.

At this point she was accustomed to answering questions that would promote discovery and point to things she already knew but hadn't really realized before. She started to miss her coach and wondered if she shouldn't call her up again.

But her situation was very different. No coaching questions, however relevant, could create knowledge for Rachel where no knowledge existed. She considered getting guidance from her regional denominational office. Their solutions tended to be the one-size-fits-all variety for churches of all sizes and styles. She knew before she called that their information would not really help her in this new church on the innovative edge. She had experience spending so much time customizing a one-size-fits-all denominational program so that it would work in her church that it didn't resemble the original program much. So she wondered why she didn't just create it herself from scratch. But she was at a bit of a loss at this point, so she called the denominational office anyway.

Much to her surprise, the person she talked with had been trained as a coach. Instead of offering an ill-fitting solution, the ministry coach asked Rachel questions about her specific situation and background. The coach even asked her about her preferred learning style and what resources she might be able to access to learn more about what could be done for her congregation.

At only a couple points in the conversation, when Rachel was at a total loss, did the ministry coach point her to a list of resources that other pastors in similar situations had found helpful. The rest would be up to Rachel. By the time the coaching session was over, Rachel had a concrete plan for how to start gaining knowledge for her project. The ministry coach at the regional office offered to follow up with Rachel and have a series of coaching sessions about how to apply her newly acquired knowledge so that she could customize her plan to suit her specific congregation.

Wow, what a switch! Denominational consultants used to try to give her all the answers and almost sounded like used-car salesmen trying to get her to buy something she wasn't sure she wanted or needed. Those interactions would leave her with thoughts that their ideas probably weren't grounded in reality, wouldn't work in her situation, and made her regret calling in the first place. This time was different! Although the coach asked questions instead of giving answers, Rachel left the interaction feeling validated, supported, wanting to learn, ready to tackle her new project, and amazed that she was already planning to participate in the follow-up coaching calls. The most memorable part of the conversation came when the ministry coach said, "The solution *you* develop will be the best one for *your* congregation."

The "Knowledge Model" on page 79 provides an illustration that helps most people see the connection between learning and coaching and why coaching really works.[1] The model works with four types of knowledge—what you know you know (KK), what you know you don't know (KDK), what you don't know that you don't know (DKDK), and what you don't know that you know (DKK). Most people are pretty content when they are in the "Know that you Know" mode (KK). These days we don't stay in the KK state long before something new comes along that we need to know. People are even

Knowledge Model

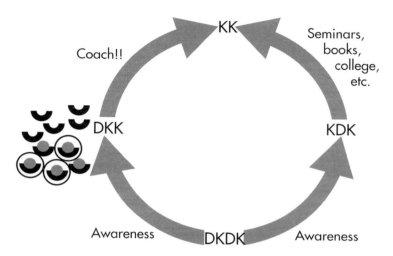

pretty content in the "Don't Know that you Don't Know" mode (DKDK). Nothing has prompted them to acquire new information, a sort of "ignorance is bliss" mode. But the awareness of knowledge that you "Know you Don't Know" (KDK) is a motivation to learn, to acquire knowledge. This usually happens when a need occurs, usually a new situation, and you realize you don't know what to do about it.

The first thing most people do when they realize they need knowledge that they do not have is to begin to search for that knowledge externally—asking people, reading books, attending seminars, taking courses. But you can take another path, an internal resource—the "Don't Know that you Know" (DKK) path. Internal resources allow you to look deep inside at experiences and knowledge that may be deeply buried because you haven't used it in a very long time or because you have had no need to connect it in ways that apply to your current situation.

Think of your brain as a collection of containers or cups (as in the diagram.) The dots represent disparate pieces of information that have been stored. A coach can help ask discovery questions to help you "connect the dots" for new learning. The coach helps you discover those internal resources. A coach helps you look inside yourself for the answers. A *Christ-Centered* coach also encourages you to utilize not only all of what God has given you but also the inspiration from the Holy Spirit to catapult learning for you.

Why take that path instead of the external?

- Greater retention
- Custom fit
- Time
- Money

You may well need to turn to external sources to fill in the gaps of your knowledge; however, if you begin by determining the internal knowledge resources you already have, you will find that the internal path is a shortcut to knowledge. It is much faster than taking a course or even reading a book. And the payoff is much greater for your investment.

The average person retains 20–40 percent of what is learned from external sources a year after the learning occurs. If the knowledge is not used and applied, the retention rate is even less. But knowledge based on internal resources is retained at 60–80 percent.

Benefits of Coaching

Coaching Others		God-Sized Goals
Intentional Progress		
Clarity/Focus	Confidence	**Learning**
Orienting around Strengths		

I used the Knowledge Model frequently at IBM to explain this benefit of coaching, but it applies equally well to ministry leaders. Churches are different; people are different. Solutions need to match the situations, and often you have much of what you need within yourself–buried in past experiences and learning.

Even when you must add new external learning, you will want to take the internal path first. If you explore your internal resources, you can more precisely determine the gaps in what you need to know and target external learning to meet your exact needs. This way you are filling in knowledge gaps and continuing to connect what you already know with the new information you are learning. Then you can easily apply both internal and external knowledge to solve the problems at hand. We need to be careful to acknowledge exactly where that knowledge originated, or this can sound like we don't need God at all. Quite the contrary, God is the giver of knowledge and the one who gave the capacity to learn.

Joining internal and external knowledge may be called catapulting learning. Such learning has two parts—awareness and actions.

Awareness

Awareness comes with the realization that you don't know something—that "aha" experience of sudden realization. Knowledge is a kind of power. This is not new. Scripture has a lot to say about knowledge and wisdom. To love the Lord with all your strength, you continually have to reinforce your strengths through learning.

The Knowledge Model is at work in every *Christ-Centered* coaching conversation. In fact, it is often the realization that you don't know what to do that drives you to talk with a coach in the first place. The best coaching starts with promoting discovery of what is already accessible in your brain and then moving on to a targeted search for external resources, programs, or seminars to fill in the gaps where you lack knowledge. But coaching doesn't stop once you have begun to determine what you know and to move toward external resources to fill in the gaps. Coaching continues in this ongoing Knowledge Model process to help you apply the learning for effective forward progress.

You've heard the age-old question: Is leadership a natural gift you're born with, or is it learned? The answer, of course, is both. The answer is "both" because you have to learn leadership skills on top of the leadership strengths you were born with. We can all recall examples of people who "used to be" great leaders. Learning leadership skills has to be a lifelong journey. The Knowledge Model might lead you to believe that learning is a planned event that happens only as a result of our initiative. But you are always learning. The brain is changing daily. Learning is a positive experience that allows you to make shifts, to adjust to your environment, to your current set of needs.

To understand more about why *Christ-Centered* coaching works and how powerful it can be, how it connects with learning, and to further understand the Knowledge Model, you need to understand more about how the brain works. (Now we're also touching on the part of the Great Commandment in Mark 12 that says to love the Lord with all your mind.)

John J. Ratey, M.D., author of *A User's Guide to the Brain*, points out that the brain functions by creating connections between neurons.[2] "Genes and environment interact to continually change the brain, from the time we are conceived until the moment we die. Our own free will may be the strongest force directing the development of our brains, and therefore our lives."[3] "The connections guide our bodies and behaviors, even as every thought and action we take physically modifies their patterns."[4] "The more firing that occurs across a specific connection, the stronger that pathway becomes."[5] "Neurons that fail to get enough signals from their target cells undergo cell death."[6] "What we do moment by moment greatly influences how the web continually reweaves itself."[7]

"Rather than using the predicative logic of a microchip, the brain is an analog processor, meaning, essentially, that it works by analogy and metaphor."[8] No wonder Jesus' parables made and still make such an impact; they are congruent with how the brain works.

"Like a set of muscles, it responds to use and disuse by either growing and remaining vital or decaying, and thus, for the first time, we are learning to see mental weaknesses as physical systems in need of training and practice."[9]

"We do have free will, in a sense, for everything we do affects everything that follows, and the brain develops in a largely unpredictable way. Genetics are important but not determinative, and the kinds of exercise, sleep, diet, friends, and activities we choose, as well as the goals we set for ourselves, have perhaps equal power to change our lives. Neurological self-awareness is the most important first step we can take."[10]

I like to think in images or metaphors. Let me share an image of the brain at work that comes from my husband, Tom. Tom's analogy is that the brain is like the paint shelf in the garage. Every time something around the house gets painted, the can of leftover paint goes to the paint shelf in the garage, just in case we ever need that color again. Every time we paint something, more cans are added to the paint shelf, so that over time that shelf gets pretty crowded. Older cans are pushed to the back of the shelf, all but forgotten. They may even be pushed off the back of the shelf because they have been unused for so long that they are crowded out by newer cans of paint.

This is a simplified way of thinking about how the brain works. New information is layered on top of the old. Old unused knowledge is buried deep beneath layers of more recently acquired knowledge. The older, long-forgotten knowledge lies buried. It's internal, lying dormant, deep within you. It can be brought to the surface again when it is needed. A coach can help you rearrange your older knowledge so that you can apply it in new situations.

Another way to envision this process is to think of an inverted pyramid or triangle standing on its point (diagram on page 83). The

Memory Structure

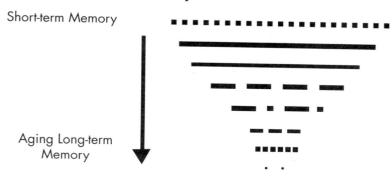

Short-term Memory

Aging Long-term
Memory

triangle is filled with parallel lines. Some of the lines are pretty solid; others are broken into shorter pieces or fragments. The pieces at the very bottom are getting squeezed out, forgotten, as new lines are added at the top. The information at the bottom is unused and may not be available for recall. The information in the middle, however, even though it is buried beneath more solid, recently acquired data, can be rearranged, connected in different ways, and reapplied. The information in short-term memory is also susceptible to being lost if not actually applied in our lives. A coach helps you move the fragments in the middle so that they can be connected near the top, where the memory is the most solid.

The brain is a "use it or lose it" system of connections. *Christ-Centered* coaching starts with the assumption that you have connections that have not been accessed in a while, and it helps you reconnect with the knowledge that you already have to keep you from losing it altogether. Even something you have learned recently, something in your short-term memory, if not used will soon be lost. If you use the information, it becomes more permanent and moves into long-term memory, where it can more likely be accessed again.

If you read a book or go to a class to learn something new, but don't connect that newly gained information in a way in which you will actually use it frequently, you will just lose those connections and will have wasted time and probably also money. Our brain works through analogy and metaphor. It is, simplistically, a pattern-matching system. But not just any patterns. It matches new concepts to which you are exposed to patterns of knowledge that you already have, and to things that you have already experienced. Coaching facilitates customized learning because the coach poses questions grounded in knowing who you are and how you think and learn. Instead of trying to force new concepts that have no match at all into your brain, coaching finds–through discovery questioning–a fit for the new concept within the context of what was already there. When you have a customized fit like that, the connections remain strong, and you retain the information for use for much longer.

I generally don't like to connect this type of *Christ-Centered* coaching with athletics, but similarities are obvious when we talk about brain function. Coaching is like having a personal trainer for the connections in your brain, so that you continually are exercising those muscles and continuing to strengthen the brain connections for future use.

When your coach asks you a question and you have to pause a minute before answering, you are actually navigating through connections looking for an answer. When that happens, you know that you are learning and likely would not have had that learning experience had it not been for the discovery question you were just asked. Rarely can you find that type of learning experience in other ways.

We retain knowledge better when we find it ourselves and create new analogies. Then, because we are applying it, it sticks like a suction cup on a clean window.

When a coach helps you discover internal resources, you will feel validation for the resources you already have that help you meet the needs of your current situation. Because you then can target specifically the new knowledge you want to acquire, you will feel affirmed that you can learn and that new learning is relevant to what you already know and can apply directly to your need. You will be able to use more of your skills. You will connect what you know in innovative ways to go in new directions to address current opportunities. And all this leads to your making greater contributions, becoming even more valuable in the Kingdom, and ultimately loving the Lord with all your strength.

The Right Questions

Still you may wonder what makes this work as a valid method for learning. When you are being coached, your coach listens to you intently and will then ask you specific questions directed at helping you make those new knowledge connections.

Good questions for a *Christ-Centered* coach to use in exploring internal knowledge are nonleading questions–questions that do not imply or point to an answer in the brain of the inquirer—but questions that cause you to spend time thinking and searching for the answer. An extreme example of a leading question is one my grandmother used to ask me when I was a little girl, "Wouldn't you like to help your mother wash the dishes?" Eventually I learned that there was only one right answer to that question. This is not the type of question your coach will ask to help you find internal knowledge.

Remember that catapulted learning is not the first benefit you acquire in a *Christ-Centered* coaching relationship. Many other benefits are already at play by the time you get to this point, so by now you already have a trusting relationship with your coach, particularly around confidentiality. If you did not, you might see a possibility that your explorations and answers might be shared with others. Then you would probably have a difficult time digging deep through your brain connections.

A coach is objective. Sometimes the best coach for you is someone who is outside your situation. I insist on having a *Christ-Centered* coach, but the coach for a ministry leader does not necessarily need to be someone who went to seminary or someone who has worked in a ministerial role. Having some distance from your profession actually helps a coach see your situation through a different lens. That different perspective helps the coach ask questions from a different direction that will also help you see in new ways. To answer the nonleading questions, you will have to think about past experiences and knowledge to see what they have to offer in current applications. The coach's questions will lead you to use knowledge you may not have accessed for a long time.

An outsider's perspective can also mean that the coach has to ask some questions just to understand your situation. That might not prompt discovery in you at all, but if you are a person who solves problems best by verbalizing them, simply explaining the situation to your coach may help you connect the dots and apply your resources.

If, however, you prefer a coach with a similar background, you may find benefits there as well. The best coach for you might be someone who has experienced some of the same things that you have because understanding your context can help the coach get right to the heart of the matter quickly with precise, on-target discovery questions. The liability of having a coach with a ministry leader's background is that the coach might tend to slip into a consulting role or to ask leading questions. Even a *Christ-Centered* coach with the same background may share your blind spots.

Equity of Exchange

Another dynamic at play on this topic of creating awareness is "equity of exchange." We all are subconsciously evaluating each person we are in conversation with, looking for the possibility of an "equity of exchange." If we think we see such a possibility, we will share more deeply. If we don't, we will stick to superficial chit-chat. This is something that happens in a split second without our specifically thinking about it—much like the concept described in Malcolm Gladwell's book *Blink: The Power of Thinking Without Thinking*.[11]

Your *Christ-Centered* coaching relationship will go well if, from early in the relationship, you have evaluated this "equity of exchange" and have determined that you will frequently receive value from your coach. That value can be in a variety of forms:

• learning, new insights, "aha" experiences
• action plans that actually happen
• validation and encouragement
• forward progress and accomplishment of large goals that didn't seem possible before

When interviewing a coach, look for someone who will naturally get you to go beyond the surface of the conversation and someone with whom you feel comfortable sharing. You might not even be able to articulate what the coach did that made you feel like sharing. That's OK as long as it happens.

The concept of "equity of exchange" is a subconcept of "Knowledge Management Communities of Practice," which is well documented in the field of knowledge management. For more information on this, consult the *Idiot's Guide to Knowledge Management*.[12]

You can expect that a *Christ-Centered* coach will be constantly aware of the need to give you value in the coaching conversation so that you will respond by searching hard for new awareness to have the most productive learning experience. The benefits described in this book are part of that value—quite a gift.

However, Jesus is the ultimate model for us on how important "equity of exchange" is in relationships. The gift he gave in sacrificing his life for our salvation is of such great value that we could spend our lives offering back ourselves and not match it. In the "equity of exchange" assessment that any of us would make, Jesus will always have given greater value, and that facilitates the deepest of relationships. He said it like this: "No one has greater love than this, to lay down one's life for one's friends" (John 15:13).

Actions

Once awareness has been created and plans begin to develop for gathering data, internal and external, your awareness is heightened. The brain connections are solidified, preparing you for action—the whole point of acquiring knowledge.

You can expect that at some point in your coaching sessions, your *Christ-Centered* coach will ask you what action you will take. If you don't want to take action, coaching may not be the thing for you.

When you design actions for yourself, even if they aren't the perfect solution to start with, you will learn. You will solidify the connections to the newly created awareness and create new capabilities for yourself. Don't expect your coach to tell you what to do; that would solidify the connections in the coach's brain but not in yours. That's not the purpose of the coaching relationship. The goal is to help *you,* the person being coached, to catapult your learning and to take action based on that acquired knowledge.

Much of what has been written about the postmodern church references the postmodern preference for experiential learning. Perhaps *Christ-Centered* coaching is the missing link to further enable the postmodern church to reach the masses of people who need to know Christ and find relationship with him.

The Greek word for *disciple* means "learner." In light of what we now know about the connection between coaching and learning, "Go...and make disciples of all nations" (Matthew 28:19) takes on a new meaning for me. I hear Jesus commissioning me to go and use coaching skills to facilitate learning about Jesus in ways customized to each and every culture—even corporate culture.

Continual and *customized* learning that comes as a result of coaching is definitely on the path to loving the Lord with all (continual) your (customized) strength.

Wisdom from the Word

Jesus was a master at creating awareness. He used language to help people think—both those who heard him in person and those who read his words today. Each of the methods he used to create awareness was structured in the format that makes new information more readily accepted by our brains. The one who created us knew that parable and metaphor would be powerful teaching tools because that's how he created our brains to operate!

He used metaphors and similes to create awareness.

The metaphor of becoming like a child:

> "Truly I tell you, unless you change and become like children, you will never enter the kingdom of heaven." (Matthew 18:3)

The comparison to accounting:

> After telling Peter to forgive, not seven times, but seventy-seven times, Jesus told the parable of the unforgiving servant:

> "For this reason the kingdom of heaven may be compared to a king who wished to settle accounts with his slaves." (Matthew 18:23)

The image of laborers in the vineyard:

> "For the kingdom of heaven is like a landowner who went out early in the morning to hire laborers for his vineyard." (Matthew 20:1)

In these and many other examples, Jesus used a familiar image to teach new truths. His images usually turned in unexpected directions to create awareness of the concepts he was trying to teach and to cause people to continue to think about the new images he created.

He used parables to create awareness.

Among his many parables, one follows the image created in the simile just given in Matthew 20:1. The story continues:

> "After agreeing with the laborers for the usual daily wage, he sent them into his vineyard. When he went out about nine o'clock, he saw others standing idle in the marketplace; and he said to them, 'You also go into the vineyard, and I will pay you whatever is right.' So they went. When he went out again about noon and about three o'clock, he did the same. And about five o'clock he went out and found others standing around; and he said to them, 'Why are you standing here idle all day?' They said to him, 'Because no one has hired us.' He said to them, 'You also go into the vineyard.' When evening came, the owner of the vineyard said to his manager, 'Call the laborers and give them their pay, beginning with the last and then going to the first.' When those hired about five o'clock came, each of them received the usual daily wage.

Now when the first came, they thought they would receive more; but each of them also received the usual daily wage. And when they received it, they grumbled against the landowner, saying, 'These last worked only one hour, and you have made them equal to us who have borne the burden of the day and the scorching heat.' But he replied to one of them, 'Friend, I am doing you no wrong; did you not agree with me for the usual daily wage? Take what belongs to you and go; I choose to give to this last the same as I give to you. Am I not allowed to do what I choose with what belongs to me? Or are you envious because I am generous?' So the last will be first, and the first will be last." (Matthew 20:2–16)

Jesus used miracles to create awareness.

One example is recorded in John 6:3–14:

Jesus went up the mountain and sat down there with his disciples. Now the Passover, the festival of the Jews, was near. When he looked up and saw a large crowd coming toward him, Jesus said to Philip, "Where are we to buy bread for these people to eat?" He said this to test him, for he himself knew what he was going to do. Philip answered him, "Six months' wages would not buy enough bread for each of them to get a little. One of his disciples, Andrew, Simon Peter's brother, said to him, "There is a boy here who has five barley loaves and two fish. But what are they among so many people?" Jesus said, "Make the people sit down." Now there was a great deal of grass in the place; so they sat down, about five thousand in all. Then Jesus took the loaves, and when he had given thanks, he distributed them to those who were seated; so also the fish, as much as they wanted. When they were satisfied, he told his disciples, "Gather up the fragments left over, so that nothing may be lost." So they gathered them up, and from the fragments of the five barley loaves, left by those who had eaten, they filled twelve baskets. When the people saw the sign that he had done, they began to say, "This is indeed the prophet who is to come into the world."

Jesus even created awareness with his body language.

He bent over and wrote, as in this Scripture passage:

They said this to test him, so that they might have some charge to bring against him. Jesus bent down and wrote with his finger on the ground. When they kept on questioning him, he straightened up and said to them, "Let anyone among you who is without sin be the first to throw a stone at her." (John 8:6–7)

In John 13, Jesus washed the disciples' feet:

"[Jesus] got up from the table, took off his outer robe, and tied a towel around himself. Then he poured water into a basin and began to wash the disciples' feet and to wipe them with the towel that was tied around him" (vv. 4–5).

In Matthew 8, he touched a leper:

There was a leper who came to him and knelt before him, saying, "Lord, if you choose, you can make me clean." He stretched out his hand and touched him, saying, "I do choose. Be made clean!" (vv. 2–3)

Again he used touch to teach when he welcomed the children:

Jesus said, "Let the little children come to me, and do not stop them; for it is to such as these that the kingdom of heaven belongs." And he laid his hands on them and went on his way. (Matthew 19:14–15)

In each of these examples, Jesus created new awareness for the listeners. But Jesus did not create the same lesson for every listener. Part of the power of the use of language in this way is that the same language can create a different learning for each individual listener based on what he or she already knows. Jesus knew this and modeled it masterfully. *Christ-Centered* coaches can use similar approaches to facilitate your learning. For that reason coaching is particularly effective in a team setting. Each team member could gain a different awareness from the same powerful question. The resulting learning would then multiply the benefit for the good of the team.

To solidify learning, action is required. Jesus also modeled this aspect of learning. When he went home with Zacchaeus, Zacchaeus found salvation. As a result of this encounter with Jesus, Zacchaeus gave half of his possessions to the poor and repaid fourfold those he had defrauded. This was Zacchaesus's action plan; it was not a directive Jesus gave him (see Luke 19:1–10).

But sometimes Jesus did suggest actions to take. In John 5, he healed a man at the temple gate. First, he said to the man, "Stand up, take your mat and walk" (v. 8). Later he said to the man, "Do not sin any more, so that nothing worse happens to you" (v. 14). Jesus knew the man could walk, but the man had to take action before he could believe it. Jesus left the decision to act up to him. Having been healed, the man could no longer be a helpless beggar; he had to be accountable for his actions. He had greater opportunities and also more responsibility.

In talking with the woman at the well (John 4), Jesus used action to engage the woman. First he asked her, "Give me a drink" (v. 7). Later he told her, "Go, call your husband, and come back" (v. 16). Using action and metaphor, Jesus got the woman's attention. She found salvation that day, and, "many Samaritans from that city believed in him because of the woman's testimony" (v. 39). As a result of her "aha" moment and what she learned, she took action and accepted Jesus' offer for living water, the kind of water he offered, promising her that she would never thirst again. She believed he was indeed the Messiah. Believing in him, she found forgiveness of sins and eternal life. Her action plan required her to tell others about the Messiah, showing that as a result of what had happened to her she loved the Lord with all her strength.

Tips for *Christ-Centered* Coaches

- You are going to want to read more about how the brain works. Look for materials written in laymen's terms that speak specifically to adult learning processes. Not only is it fascinating reading, but you'll be a better coach when you understand more about what's going on with the person you are coaching when you are having to wait for an answer to a great question. It will help you facilitate those "ahas" more readily.
- The ability to consistently ask discovery questions takes practice. Each time you ask a great coaching question, new connections are made in your own brain as to how to create the type of question that produces learning. The more you do it, the more that connection is strengthened for you. That's why professional certification requires many hours of having worked with clients, and not just having read about how to coach.
- The use of metaphor, parable, and story are advanced coaching skills. The more you learn to use these skills, the more impact you will have in facilitating learning and results because of the analog processing that is inherent in brain function.

Tips for Working with a *Christ-Centered* Coach

- Let go of not wanting to admit that you don't already know something. Trying to impress your coach with what you already know is counterproductive to the learning experience that a *Christ-Centered* coaching session can be.
- Come to coaching sessions with an attitude of wanting to learn something new. If you do, you will. You won't necessarily learn *from* your coach, but *because of* your coach.
- Take care of yourself. Sleep, diet, and exercise all play roles in your ability to learn and strengthen brain connections. When you do that, you create the best environment for your coaching sessions to be great learning sessions.

CHAPTER 8

Christ-Centered Coaching Fosters Intentional Progress

Do not neglect the gift that is in you...Put these things into practice, devote yourself to them, so that all may see your progress.
1 TIMOTHY 4:14A, 15

One month Frank was a pastor, a really good one. The next month he had oversight responsibilities for 150 pastors in his region. To say he felt overwhelmed would be an understatement of how he felt in his new position after only a few weeks of doing it.

Other than the regional meeting at which he was affirmed in the position, when many of the pastors were present, he had only gotten to interact with each pastor one at a time. He wondered if it was even possible to see each pastor once a year. More often than that, unless the contact came at regional meetings, it definitely seemed impossible. How could he develop relationships with people he could spend quality time with only once a year?

Looking for answers and at least a little reassurance, he called his friend Joe, who held the same job in another state. That conversation left him feeling more discouraged than before.

Joe said that in this role the only way to manage was by "the squeaky wheel gets the grease" method. Churches in conflict or pastors who had some kind of critical need got attention. You just didn't worry about ministry leaders and churches that didn't have conflict or other critical needs.

Frank wondered about someone who might be like the Tin Man from *The Wizard of Oz,* having so many challenges for so long that he had no way even to squeak. Or what about pastors who were like he had been, pretty successful but feeling like a loner needing some kind of support. Wasn't he supposed to shepherd them, too?

The challenge seemed too big.

Then one of the more successful pastors in his region mentioned something about having a coach who was helping him tremendously. Frank asked for contact information and gave the coach a call.

Frank was pleased that his coach didn't seem intimidated by the magnitude of his challenges. Very methodically Frank built a certain amount of momentum by identifying his strengths, developing clarity and focus around his calling, and gaining confidence with a steep learning curve. All this happened relatively quickly, at least quicker than he had anticipated; and he enjoyed the relationship with the coach. But the challenges remained formidable.

Frank discovered that a key thing that still had him stuck was that conversation with Joe back when he first started. Joe had more experience than he did, so Frank believed that Joe should know what he was talking about. And Joe wasn't the only one! As he met more of his peers, Frank heard the same story all over. That served to confirm his beliefs that he had few options.

The breakthrough for Frank came one day in a coaching session. Frank conveyed to his coach his unhappiness with the results he was seeing in his region. He attributed this to the fact that he couldn't really develop high-quality relationships with the pastors in the way he wanted.

His coach asked for more information. "Tell me more about your interactions with the pastors."

"All the interactions are infrequent and brief. With so many pastors, I can't really develop an in-depth relationship with any of them. I just don't have the time. I haven't even been able to talk with all the pastors even once."

"How could you design your interactions differently to get the results you want?"

Frank was stumped. "I've wracked my brain on this. I don't think it's possible. This job is just way over my head."

"What makes you think it is impossible?"

Frank described his conversations with Joe and others. "The other ministers in a position like this have told me that this is the only way this job can be done. They've done their jobs this way for years. I don't know what would make me believe I can come up with anything better."

"Frank, I think that's the key. You have convinced yourself that there's only one way to do this job. Holding on to that belief may be holding you back from finding a better way."

"When I first started, I believed I could do just that—find a better way. But over time I've stopped believing that I can improve on what I've been told."

"What would you have to believe instead?"

"I guess I'd have to believe that I can find a totally new way to approach this role that no one has ever attempted before."

"Great! With that belief, what behaviors that you've never tried before could you start to do?"

Frank began to talk about a number of innovative ideas that he'd been thinking about for several months. He reluctantly admitted that he had just not given them much thought because of his belief that his ideas were too radically different from what his peers had told him. That belief had pretty much stopped his progress.

"How would each of these new ideas impact your relationships with your pastors?"

Frank's voice began to show his excitement. As he described the ideas to his coach, he could see that the ideas really did have a good chance of making a positive impact on his relationships with the pastors. He could already imagine that the results in his region might be different.

Before the session was over, Frank noticed that the key turning point in his conversation had been in realizing that one of his beliefs was limiting his progress.

His coach offered one more thought: "May I suggest something for you to think about?"

"Of course."

"Just think about this. I don't necessarily want you to answer this today. What other limiting beliefs might be getting in your way?"

Over time Frank tried his ideas one by one. Some worked, and some didn't; but he was no longer stuck believing that change in the way he did his job was impossible. He was making a lot more progress. The momentum seemed to be building even faster.

When he looked back on the coaching relationship, Frank realized that one of the best outcomes was being intentional in developing strategies to deal with challenges one at a time. Synergy of successes in tackling the challenges by taking specific actions pointed to real forward progress. Frank became focused and created leapfrog, exponential progress instead of plodding progress that only left him feeling frustrated and frazzled.

Benefits of Coaching

Coaching Others	God-Sized Goals
Intentional Progress	

Clarity/Focus	Confidence	Learning
Orienting around Strengths		

Making Progress

Once you've experienced enough benefits with *Christ-Centered* coaching to start making progress, even more elements can contribute to increased progress. These elements involve intentional strategies on your part. We'll look at each of these:

• The Results Cycle
• Accountability
• Personal Systems
• The Habit of Shifting
• The Heart of the Matter
• Planning and Goal Setting

The Results Cycle

*Diagram adapted and used with permission from *The Heart of Coaching* by Thomas G. Crane, FTA Press: 858-487-9017, www.craneconsulting.com*

The Results Cycle

Frank experienced "The Results Cycle" model up close and personal. The coach heard two key parts:

1. Results were not what he wanted.
2. Relationships were not at the quality level he wanted.

The conversation pointed to one of many coaching models coaches use to forward the conversation. This one is from *The Heart of Coaching* by Thomas G. Crane.[1] It is not uncommon for people to get stuck by their limiting beliefs. You may want to think about the same question that Frank needed to consider: What beliefs are currently limiting you?

Even if you know your strengths, are clear and focused, confident, and continually learning, you still might not be experiencing any forward motion, any real gains on the vision you are trying to claim. Many people are motivated to act. Still, acquiring skills and knowledge and determining what they want to do offer no guarantee of actually seeing the action plan become reality. The remaining problem lies in the knowing versus doing gap.

You may have figured out what you need to do, but you just don't do it. How can *Christ-Centered* coaching help you put your plan into action?

Accountability

The goal in coaching is not to make the person being coached accountable to the coach. Rather, the *Christ-Centered* coach helps a person be accountable to himself or herself.

Being accountable to oneself is difficult. It may even be especially difficult to ministry leaders. Here's how this might play itself out. You resolve to take small actions. You promise yourself that you'll take a well-deserved night off on Thursday. Then you get a call that the finance committee would really like you to attend a meeting that night. You promise yourself that you'll go to the gym on Tuesday afternoon, and then you find out your son has a ball game at the same time. You promise yourself you'll start your diet on Sunday, and then the student group insists that you stay after church for their pizza party. You promise yourself that you will take new actions to fulfill your purpose, to expand your ministry, to reach a new level. Instead, you respond to other people's needs and don't keep your promise to yourself. You may be doing good things, but you may not be doing the best things to take your ministry where you believe God wants it to go.

Having a *Christ-Centered* coach helps people become self-accountable. Giving yourself a break from keeping your commitments to yourself or putting yourself last becomes demoralizing over time. Continually failing to keep your promises to yourself chips away at your self-trust. Just as breaking a promise to another erodes trust in a relationship, breaking a promise to yourself destroys confidence. You will begin to think you are not capable of the discipline needed to achieve your goals. But a coach can help you develop a habit of keeping your promises to yourself.

Ultimately your accountability is to God, of course. When you break promises to yourself, you usually also hurt your relationship with God because breaking promises to God is a lot like breaking them to yourself. No one knows but you and God.

Before you stop and begin to berate yourself for breaking those promises to yourself, keep in mind that everyone is guilty. It's easy to break promises to yourself. After all, no one knows, and you are often making a choice to put others first. But that kind of flexibility can lead to your stagnation in making progress on the purpose God intends you to fulfill. Having a *Christ-Centered* coach gives you an accountability partner. A coach is not your mother. A coach isn't going to tell you what to do or scold you if you don't make progress on the action plan you created for yourself, but a coach will know if you did what you said you would do, because you have told the coach you would do it.

One of the things that contributes to this benefit of making intentional progress is the accountability system established between you and your coach. What I really mean by the statement, "A coach is not your mother," is that you are an adult. If you tell me you are going to take a particular action, I will assume you are either going to do it or you will have some valid reason for not doing it. Since I'm assuming you are an adult with good judgment, I know you are capable of keeping your promise to yourself, and I will gladly be your accountability partner in the process. I will not hound you to make sure you do what you said you are going to do; that's your job. But having an accountability relationship with your coach really helps most people do what they say they will do.

Intentional change is significant for adults who are on a treadmill of routine. Often adults haven't learned anything significant to apply to their lives, and they haven't made any big changes in a long time. One day is pretty much like the one before and the next one. Because they have done the same things in the same way for so long they often don't have the systems in place to facilitate learning or to discipline themselves to remember commitments to themselves. Making significant change takes a lot of intentional, focused effort.

A *Christ-Centered* coach actually doesn't have to worry much about checking up on you because you will experience your own consequences for not taking the action. You will either remain stuck where you are as a result of your inactivity, or the situation will become worse. In either case, the results you experience will likely appear as a topic for a future coaching conversation. Then your coach can talk with you about the barriers that stopped you from taking the action in the first place.

You may be wondering how accountability in a *Christ-Centered* coaching relationship works to provide the benefit of intentional progress. Simply speaking out loud to another human being often creates just enough incentive to follow through with your action plan. Talking about what you will do out loud with your coach clarifies the steps you want to take, helps you establish a time line, keeps your mind focused on your goals and the vision that is within reach, and solidifies the reasons for taking this action. Your act of voicing what you want to do will increase your excitement about the potential results of your action. You will actually motivate yourself to follow through with your commitment. Your coach will support you in being accountable to yourself.

If you habitually break promises to yourself, you may need to stop and work with your coach to figure out how you can develop a stronger sense of self so that you see yourself as worthy of keeping promises to yourself. Don't worry, we're not talking about therapy here, only identifying barriers and then designing actions to overcome them. Though I have no magic formulas to help you do that, a coach can often see patterns in your behavior when you describe what happened during your week to keep you from following through with what you planned to do. By looking at those patterns, together you can plan what you can do in similar circumstances to overcome your barriers.

Barriers to following through on your plan of action have a common theme. The need to address them and to move on with your own plans is like an emergency on an airplane when you must put on your oxygen mask first before being able to help someone else. At some point ministry leaders need to realize that to help others make progress in their lives, leaders must first follow through on their own action plans. You must value yourself enough to keep promises to yourself. A large part of ministry involves taking care of others and leading others in ministry. It is much easier to come alongside them and help them keep their commitments when your own life gives evidence of that kind of discipline.

The specifics of taking care of yourself by honoring your promises to yourself take different shapes for different people. For some, the new discipline means getting more rest, exercising regularly, eating well, being kind to yourself when you make mistakes, or allowing yourself to have personal goals and following through to make those goals reality. Taking care of yourself physically is a good place to start in keeping promises to yourself. Your improved physical condition will make you feel better—more positive about yourself—and actually help you keep other commitments to yourself. When you follow through on one promise to yourself, you'll find that it is easier to keep other promises to yourself as well.

If you don't learn to make and keep commitments to yourself, you are much more susceptible to falling into bad habits. And if you keep commitments only because you promised your coach you would do so, then once the *Christ-Centered* coaching relationship ends, you are not likely to continue to keep those promises to yourself. Keeping promises only because of a relationship with your coach instead of because you value yourself enough to keep self-promises is not healthy. Your relationship with your coach is simply creating codependency.

Personal Systems

Beyond accountability, a second thing that helps bridge the knowing versus doing gap is having personal systems in place for getting things done. This is very customized to the challenges you have and how you would best be supported. There is no single magic pill or prescription. A *Christ-Centered* coach can help you develop and put into practice the personal systems for taking action.

Personal systems are ways to organize your day and your progress. Different people like different systems. Some people do well prioritizing the way they spend their time by using to-do lists. Others find that putting due dates on calendars, Post-it™ notes on computers, or entering everything into a handheld computer works best. You might talk with your coach about the system you use and what works best for you. Simply having a system in place can help you keep your commitments just by organizing your life, having a plan, and keeping your priorities visible. However, having a system is not an automatic solution, especially if you just won't keep commitments you have made to yourself.

If you're wondering exactly what examples of those systems are, it may be because you don't have much of a system in place. Consider these questions: How do you assign to-dos to yourself and make sure that you do them? What strategies do you use to deal with demands for your time and energy such as e-mail, phone calls, mail, invitations to a variety of nonessential meetings, and time consumers? Notice that some of the incessant demands on our time are electronic. The ubiquitous cell phone and "you've got mail" invade your space and can consume your day.

As I've worked with ministry leaders on these topics, they have determined that they want to behave differently. Some of the actions they have identified for themselves have been: to limit how many times a day they check their e-mail, to turn off their cell phone so that they can get prioritized work accomplished, to develop realistic estimates of how much time their routine tasks require and plan accordingly, and to control their time instead of allowing the impositions on their time to control what they get done each day. In each of these cases, the results have been significant.

If you've suddenly realized you have no personal plan for prioritizing your time, you may want to check out some of the many available resources. A good one is David Allen's *Getting Things Done.*[2] It has a rather prescriptive example of a system, but it's a place to start. The most important thing, though, is to develop a system that works for you.

Whatever system you choose requires that you know your values. It has often been said your checkbook and your calendar tell quickly what you truly value. You may say that you value your family above all else, but if every date you make with a family member is set aside for a ministry task, your actions show that your true values are different from what you say they are. If you say you value saving for your kids' education, but you haven't put any money aside for that purpose in years, your real values don't match up with what you say.

Are your checkbook and calendar accurate reflections of what you say you value? If you discover a mismatch, you have just found a good topic for a coaching session. You can talk about how to get what you say you value and where you spend your time and money into better alignment.

If you have just had an "aha" moment, realizing a mismatch in your calendar or checkbook with what you say you value, you are not alone. This is true in some degree for everyone—not just ministers, not just laypeople. Everyone has some individual issues—a spending habit they'd like to change, a time waster they'd like to get under control. The gap between where you are and where you want to be comes up when progress is not being made. This is a thread that runs throughout your coaching experience, but the benefit shows up here because your momentum is building. When you are testing to see if your momentum is really increasing and you want the results you envision to become reality, you become increasingly aware of what's holding you back. The progress you make, the pace of getting to this point, is quicker for people who have workable systems in place.

I have rarely worked with anyone who didn't need to work on something related to personal systems. I've also noticed that since the person being coached sets the agenda, these are some of the first things people mention as presenting a challenge or giving them problems. However, once you have tackled and reaped the benefits of finding your strengths, gaining clarity and focus, building confidence, and learning continually, you will likely return to this spot to change the systems based on what you have learned. The benefit in *Christ-Centered* coaching is that you can go at your own pace and deal with what is most needed as you perceive it. A coaching colleague and dear friend of mine, Frank Skidmore, says, "Help is defined by the receiver." You determine the help you need, and you must be accountable for the action and progress that result.

The Habit of Shifting to Get Unstuck

It's one thing to have an initial new awareness but another actually to experience a true shift–a change in thinking accompanied by realigning behavior to conform to the new thinking. Two parts are evident: changing thinking and new actions consistent with that change of thinking. The change in thinking exercises brain muscles–neurons–making a solid piece of learning, making that learning accessible for the future. Over time the new actions resulting from the shift in thinking become a habit. Forming new habits is another benefit of how the process of coaching is congruent with how the brain works.

The more you do something–in this case, changing your thinking and realigning your actions with those changes–the stronger your brain becomes in being able to do that same thing with ease. That's a true shift.

Remember the story in chapter 5 about the man who realized that being born again was a shift? His realization came from learning how to make big shifts and doing it so often that it became habit for him. The positive results of the shifts he made created a willingness to look for shifts as a valid strategy for getting unstuck. This developed into a habit and helped him consistently make more intentional progress. He created a positive upward spiral effect by the rapidity with which he began to shift to ever-improved ways of addressing a variety of situations. When he was exposed to the concept of being born again, he was able to match that concept to a pattern of behavior that he had been developing over a period of months.

Active processes develop over time; they are not instant, moment-in-time creations. Your processes for the way you get things done go far beyond the confines of coaching conversations. If you make shifts in thinking and behavior and modify your processes, over time you will get better at it. Shifts will be increasingly easier to make because of the positive results you have experienced. You will look for new shifts to make because of the excitement of discovery and improvement you have enjoyed. The reward you experience is something you want to continue to enjoy, so shifting becomes natural, creating positive, upward spiral effects.

A similar positive spiral happens on other *Christ-Centered* coaching topics as well—

- identifying strengths that you didn't know you had and leveraging them,
- wading through the mire to gain clarity and focus to the point of insisting on having it,
- acting on your newly gained confidence,
- embarking on a learning path to go beyond what you've known before,
- developing new personal systems.

Your list will be determined by the help you need and the agenda you set with your coach.

Add all of this together, and it can equate to a habit of intentional progress. Experiencing intentional progress becomes addictive because of positive rewards.

The Heart of the Matter

Often, when progress seems to be blocked, you are dealing with the symptoms instead of the source of the problem.[3] For example, as essential as calendars, PDAs, and to-do lists are, they simply record your data. They do not prioritize your time, determine your values, or help you make progress. Continually changing your system for scheduling your time is dealing with a symptom rather than with the source of the problem—the real reason you aren't keeping commitments to yourself and aren't staying consistent with what you say you value compared with how you spend your time and money. Real progress results from dealing with the heart of the matter.

Let's take Frank as an example. When he first changed jobs, the symptoms of his frustration were that he was new at the job and the realization that it took a long time to get around to each of the pastors in his region. These symptoms were on the surface, observable data.

One approach Frank could have taken to deal with this challenge might have been to address the symptoms. Frank could have adopted the same strategy as his friend and only worked with the pastors in crisis, or he could have decided on some type of system for visiting with each pastor on an annual basis and disciplining himself to limit the amount of time with each one so that he could make it around to all of them. But addressing the source of the challenge instead of just the symptoms could open up different possibilities and enable him to come up with a much better, more permanent solution.

What was the source of the challenge? With his *Christ-Centered* coach's help, Frank discovered several. One source was that the norm of how the job had been done in the past was not going to help him get the results that he wanted. When he began the job, he had at first assumed that the norm was a given, but that assumption became an inhibitor to finding a new system for accomplishing what he envisioned—to give pastors the help they needed. To do that as he intended, he needed a totally different system.

Another source of the challenge was that he had been thinking that the purpose of his job was to supply the answers, to solve the pastors' problems. Because he had been a successful pastor, he at first assumed that his job was to ensure that all pastors had similar experiences. To do that he thought he had to be a Mr. Fix-it. It didn't take long for Frank to discover that if he became the supplier of the answers, all of the pastors in his region could only be as effective, good, or resourceful as he was. In effect, he would be creating "mini-me's," clones of himself.

Such an approach was limiting in many ways. Most ministers sincerely believe that as servant leaders they should move themselves to the background to focus on other people and their needs and to keep Jesus Christ at the forefront.[4] A gap in practice and belief becomes evident, for example, when they look at their calendar and budget and see that they are putting themselves at the forefront as problem solver, not in the background as a servant leader. They see that they have budgeted money to attend conferences; they spend their time with churches in conflict, trying to solve their problems.

Frank quickly saw that these processes would need to change if he were to help pastors develop themselves to the fullest instead of developing them to be like him. If he truly wanted pastors to reach their greatest potential, perhaps far beyond what he ever achieved, he would have to help each pastor build on his or her unique strengths and minister to the needs of his or her particular congregation. Frank realized that he needed to shift his role to one of bringing out the pastors' full Kingdom potential and helping them become and achieve more than he ever had as a pastor.

Addressing the challenge at the source, rather than the observable symptoms, not only opens up more possibilities for solutions but also helps prevent the challenge from becoming a recurring crisis. That's how the forward progress happens. Progress is made when you stop the same types of challenges from coming up. You might look like you're making progress if you address symptoms, but they will keep coming back. Such a fix isn't permanent. You might move one step forward temporarily and then take two steps back because the source is still there, not being addressed.

A *Christ-Centered* coach can help you look deeper to find the source. It's hard for us to do this for ourselves. The urgency of the moment would tend to keep us singularly focused on addressing symptoms one after the other unless someone like a coach is insisting that we slow down and take a hard look at what's happening. Getting past symptoms to discover sources on your own is difficult because you are so busy addressing symptoms over and over that you may not always recognize the symptoms as having the same source.

We also tend to address symptoms in the same way that we've always addressed similar symptoms in the past. A coach will challenge you to think creatively and develop solutions that you haven't thought of before so that the challenge of addressing the same symptoms can be eliminated by getting to the source and dealing with it.

Planning and Goal Setting

Trying to reach your goals without a plan is like getting in the car to drive and just making random turns until you get tired. Then you just stop for the day only to pick up again and do the same thing tomorrow. At some point you'll want to know where you are going.

That's a very different experience from choosing a destination, getting out a map, and developing a strategy to get there. If you want to get from Raleigh to Seattle, you can't just hop on any interstate and start driving. You will only reach your destination if you keep driving in the right direction. And you can only tell if you are making progress if you know where you are going.

Have you ever driven a car with a global positioning system (GPS)? It can be a great asset to get you where you want to go. It accurately reads your position, and once you input your destination, it quickly calculates the route to get there. Like a good coach, it may ask some questions such as, "Where would you like to go?" and help you consider multiple options such as: "Do you want to go the shortest distance, the fastest route, or the most scenic?" All three options will get you there. One may be more pleasant to see. Another may mean interstate travel and higher speeds, while another will consume fewer miles but mean a lot of stoplights along the way.

The GPS will notice when you don't take the path that is planned. I personally can't stand the brands that yell at you when you've veered from the plan. I've actually experienced some that say, "You made a wrong turn! Turn back now!" Even if I did make a wrong turn, such a GPS makes me want to yell back, "I'm the human being here. I changed my mind, and I don't have to check with you!" What's unattractive in a GPS is also unattractive in a coach. I do, however, like a GPS that notices you took a new turn and supports you in that decision by automatically calculating another path to the same destination, acknowledging that, after all, *you* are the driver. Some GPSs will even congratulate you when you arrive at your destination!

Let's look at the role of a *Christ-Centered* coach in planning and goal setting. A coach will not pick the destination, provide the map, or even dictate your strategy. After all, it's *your* ministry, and you are the expert in what God has called you to do, even if you don't yet know how to do it. A coach may not be an expert in your ministry. But a coach can help you get there by insisting that you have goals and plans. If you don't know how to plan, a coach will ask you where you can learn how to plan using the way that you learn best. A coach will also be your thought partner throughout the process of developing those goals and the plans for achieving them.

Without a plan of action, a coach could talk to you about your strengths and how to maximize them. You could have clarity about your call and focus on actions. You could address fears and become confident, and you could be constantly learning, but you would still be like the Israelites wandering in the desert. Wandering does not feel like progress.

Most of us understand that concept and want to move forward. We often embark on the task to establish goals and put plans in place to achieve them. But how many times have you thought of goals and plans and wished that you could just bounce your ideas off someone else? Sometimes we are reluctant to do that because of what the person we are sharing with might think or because we don't want to take up their time. Or, in an extreme case, they might take your idea and make it their own. Extroverts especially need to hear themselves speak their ideas.

That's another way your *Christ-Centered* coach can help you experience the benefit of intentional progress. A coach can listen to your ideas, giving you a safe place to express your ideas and hear yourself think through all your options and possible barriers to successful progress. In this way a coach becomes a thought partner to help you develop your own road map to reach your destination. A coach is consistently listening for the positive, not for things to critique. A coach wants you to succeed, and his or her role is one of encouragement. Because coaches are nonjudgmental, they provide a safe context in which to express ideas, goals, and a plan for reaching your God-given purpose. Your coach is not interested in taking your ideas, but rather is focused on helping you successfully implement them.

Redirection is often necessary because life changes. People often don't want to put a plan into place because plans seem rigid. When change occurs, they ditch their plans instead of updating them. Plans must be created with the ability to be flexible, adjusting to each new day and the challenges it brings. The destination is still the same. The course may just shift a little. A flexible plan is much easier to live with. That way you don't have to abandon the trip because a bridge is out or there is construction on the interstate. Just adjust the route you'll take to get there.

Jesus reminded us in the Sermon on the Mount that we should not worry about tomorrow but, instead, let each day take care of itself. We have to hold each day loosely and remain open to what God will say each day. However, this does not mean we should abandon planning. Jesus also said, "For which of you, intending to build a tower, does not first sit down and estimate the cost, to see whether he has enough to complete it?" (Luke 14:28).

Goals change, and plans change. Coaches know this, even expect it. In fact, if plans and goals don't change, a coach would be curious about those goals and plans. When they change, it is a sign of your growth and progress. In working with a *Christ-Centered* coach, you can rest in the fact that your coach will go with you as your goals and plans change. Your coach is an advocate for you and your success. That is the spirit in which a coach might offer input on things that you may not be seeing—your blind spots (similar to the GPS noticing that you've taken a turn that was off course). But you, not the coach, will be the decision maker about your own next steps for course correction. The intent of a coach will not be to judge or criticize, but to uplift. Your coach celebrates with you when you succeed in reaching your destination.

Simplicity

The simplest plan is often the best. An elaborate plan may get so complicated that no one can follow it. Such goals and planning systems can actually be the culprit responsible for slowing or even stopping progress.

In working with a coach, you are encouraged to have just enough in the way of goals and planning to know where you are going and how you might get there, but not so much that you are prevented from actually moving forward.

Let's consider our trip again. Our goal is to go from Raleigh, North Carolina, to Seattle, Washington. You have several ways to get there. You may take a bus. You might try Amtrak. You could drive, or you could fly, or do a combination of the two. Depending on how much time you wanted to take, you could also bike or walk. If you mapped out all the ways to get from Raleigh to Seattle, it might take you weeks or even months. If you were set on developing a fail-safe plan for getting to Seattle that had considered every single eventuality, you could actually make a job for yourself in plotting all the permutations of how to get to Seattle. By the time you had figured out the exhaustive list of ways to get there, new roads could have been built, or new flights could have been created. Old flights that you checked on might no longer be available. The weather or seasons may have changed, making some options less desirable. When you feel you must explore every possible option, you will have so many ideas that you can't determine what you want to do. You will have expended all your energy in planning, and you'll never get to Seattle.

This analogy may seem extreme, but this very thing happens in corporations all the time. And it's not limited to corporations. It happens with individuals, in families, in small businesses, and even in churches. Sometimes making a big production out of planning is an effort, perhaps subconscious, to show just how impossible the endeavor is. If it seems difficult enough, no one will be surprised when you don't succeed. Behind extra planning can be fear, risk aversion, or a need to choose somewhere between folly and wisdom.

Ministry leaders are as guilty as anyone else. They can get stuck building elaborate plans to achieve complicated goals. A *Christ-Centered* coach will encourage you to plan while looking at your own constraints of time and resources, then to pick a strategy and act.

In working with lots of ministry leaders, I've noticed that an effective way of planning and setting goals is to try to put your plans on one page. On one page, you would list your vision, mission, objectives, strategies, and plans. If you can do that, you have clarity and focus, and you've thought through what you'd like to do so well that you now have a simple plan for getting there.

My clients were coming up with this idea long before I knew that this process is well documented by Jim Horan in his book *The One Page Business Plan*.[5] Once I read that book, I recognized it was exactly what my clients, one after the other, had been inventing for a couple of years. Their plans didn't necessarily look exactly as Jim described, but they were similar enough that it was uncanny. They had all come up with a one-page ministry plan—simple enough to fit on one page, yet elaborate enough to show what you need to do.

In Horan's book you could easily substitute the word *ministry* for *business* and develop your own one-page ministry plan. The process would be the same. Once a ministry leader starts going down this path, I find it helps fast-forward the process to read this book and then figure out if these concepts of simplicity can help.

Working with a *Christ-Centered* coach can help you bridge the knowing versus doing gap, develop the habit of getting unstuck, and put together simple goals and plans to make intentional progress in your ministry.

Progress and Strength

How does all this lead to loving the Lord with all your strength? At first the connection between loving and intentional progress might not make sense. Loving is an emotion, right? But Jesus said that you obey if you love: "If you love me, you will keep my commandments" (John 14:15). Obeying is doing, an action. You love me if you take action and if those actions align with my teachings.

It's also consistent with what Paul wrote to Timothy: "For God did not give us a spirit of cowardice, but rather a spirit of power and of love and of self-discipline" (2 Timothy 1:7). All of these are needed to make progress by taking action and reaching your God-given purpose.

Another way to say this would be that you demonstrate your love by the intentional actions you take. Progress then is what the Lord supplies as a response to the faithful actions we take that are congruent with Jesus' commands.

The alignment of knowing versus doing then involves "knowing" what Jesus commands of us and then taking action. Taking action to make progress is becoming accountable. Jesus said in John 14 that we will get help with that in the form of the Comforter who will be with us. Paul said that we will get help with accountability in the relationship found in the body of Christ and from the Bible, which is good for instruction (knowledge), correction, and reproof.

God has given us what we need to love him with all our strength. Let's not let any barrier keep us from acting in obedience to the divine will and purpose for our lives.

Help from Scripture

God's Word encourages us to do things in an orderly way:

All things should be done decently and in order.
(1 Corinthians 14:40)

We can depend on consistency from God:

Jesus Christ is the same yesterday and today and forever. (Hebrews 13:8)

We should act on what we believe:

"Be doers of the word, and not merely hearers who deceive themselves. (James 1:22)

We should always be mindful of God's good plans for us:

"For surely I know the plans I have for you, says the LORD, plans for your welfare and not for harm, to give you a future with hope. Then when you call upon me and come and pray to me, I will hear you. When you search for me, you will find me; if you seek me with all your heart, I will let you find me." (Jeremiah 29:11–14a)

Human plans must be dedicated to God:

Commit your work to the LORD,
   and your plans will be established. (Proverbs 16:3)

Tips for *Christ-Centered* Coaches

- Hold yourself to the same standard of intentional progress that you do those you would coach. To do that, you need to be working with a coach. If coaching is good for the people you coach, it's good for you, too, right? In fact, your progress can be an inspiration for their progress.
- In small ways, share your progress and challenges with those you are coaching. It helps build the relationship and open the sharing to a deeper level. This contributes to your ultimate goal for those you coach—that they will thrive and realize their full Kingdom potential. But be careful not to dominate the conversation and make it all about you.

Tips for Working with a *Christ-Centered* Coach

- Get ready to move forward! This is a mental exercise and a choice.
- Choose a route to "Seattle" and go! Next time, you can get there differently if you learn there is a better way. In the meantime you'll enjoy having arrived at your destination.

CHAPTER 9

Christ-Centered Coaching Rubs Off on Others

The gifts he gave were...to equip the saints for the work of ministry, for building up the body of Christ, until all of us come to the unity of the faith and of the knowledge of the Son of God, to maturity, to the measure of the full stature of Christ.

EPHESIANS 4:11–13

Phil was a pastor in a church situation that many would envy. His church was in a steep growth curve and moving from the status of a new church plant to an established church. But Phil was worried.

When the church was just getting started, everyone got involved and did whatever needed to be done. Excitement and contagious positive energy could be felt around the place and with any of the members. Just talking about the church generated an enthusiastic, lively conversation.

But lately, now that they were really becoming more of an established church, for some reason people stopped assuming they would need to pitch in and help. No one was saying, "Let someone else do it; I've done enough; I'm taking a break," but that certainly seemed to be what was happening. It was as if the people somehow expected things just to happen, that the work would take care of itself.

Growth was continuing at a rapid pace, so gaps in ministry areas were starting to occur. For the first time in the church's history, Phil was at a loss about filling significant volunteer gaps.

Phil was good at building relationships. That's one of the things that served the church well when they were just beginning. People were attracted to him and the relational environment that he created.

Because of those relationships, Phil recognized the great quantity of untapped potential sitting in the pews each Sunday. He felt certain that these folks were pretty successful in their careers. He knew the church greatly needed some of those same strengths that made them successful in their careers. Why could he see that, and they couldn't?

He decided this was going to be the topic of his next coaching session. He still met with the same coach who had been an invaluable asset throughout the whole process of starting this church, even when the church was just a twinkle in the eyes of four couples from the sponsoring church.

Here's how the conversation with the coach went.

"What am I going to do?" Phil asked after describing his concern.

His coach asked, "What is the current situation?"

"People expect things to happen, but they aren't getting involved to help."

"Where do you want the situation to be?" his coach continued to ask questions.

Phil explained that he wanted every member to realize full Kingdom potential. He went on to talk about his vision for the church as it continued to unfold. He talked about his goal of reaching people as well as his desire for individuals to grow as disciples so that they might find fulfillment in their place in the Kingdom as they found God's purpose in their own lives.

The coach's next question, "What can you do to bring that out?"

"I don't know. You've brought out more of my potential. I wish you could do that for the rest of the church. Can you do that?" Phil had begun to use coaching language and style and was asking questions of his own.

But his coach just came back with a question, "That's a possibility. What's another option?"

After a thoughtful pause, Phil answered, "After learning from your work with me, I think I might have some strengths as a coach. But I'm the pastor, and pastors don't coach members of their congregation."

"Really?" The coach wasn't accepting Phil's assessment of the status quo and pushed Phil to go deeper in analyzing the situation.

"Well, I don't know any who do. Besides, I'm supposed to be the one with all the answers, not the one asking the questions. I'd be afraid that if I started asking questions, it would cause people to get really nervous. They'd probably think, 'If he's asking us, we are definitely in trouble now.' It might cause them to lose respect for me." Phil was beginning to express his fears and limiting his belief in himself and his own potential.

"I'm not sure that very many people in churches today actually believe that pastors have all the answers. That doesn't mean they question your spiritual authority. There just may be other ways to be a spiritual leader without being the answer guy." Wow, the coach challenged and pushed back without asking a question!

"You're probably right about that, but they are constantly asking me what to do next as if I do have all the answers."

Back in question mode, the coach asked, "How could you test out if it would work for you to coach some of the people in your church?"

"I could coach one person, I suppose."

Thinking that Phil was wanting to continue to explore this line of thinking, the coach asked, "What might be the benefit of coaching them versus advising them?"

"All the benefits that I've experienced myself–strengths, clarity and focus, confidence, learning, intentionality–came from coaching, not from someone giving me advice. I would never have reached this level of benefits from hearing what someone else thought about my situation and doing what another person suggested."

Pressing on, the coach asked, "What would be the downside?"

"Now that I think about it, the benefits might outweigh the downside. I think what I really need is respect, and I don't really have to have all the answers to gain that. At least, I don't think I do. I might find out differently if I try it."

The conversation continued.

"Who do you think is extremely coachable?"

"I might have to think about that. But my first thought is the current leader of the neighborhood ministries team, Sam."

"When might you be able to coach this person?"

"I already have a meeting scheduled with him later this week."

"Great. How will you start?"

"I'll go back to my notes and tell him some of the same things you told me when we first got started and go from there. I have a good relationship with Sam, so I think I can just say that I think coaching might be a better way to address his challenges and ask if we can try even though I'm new at it."

"Great. I can't wait to hear what happens."

Not only did Phil's coaching relationship with Sam work well, but over time it also worked with all the team leaders. In a few cases Phil even coached whole teams and not just the leader.

Phil began to get comments from parishioners that they really respected him for putting his own agenda aside and helping them to realize their own Kingdom potential individually and as a part of the body. In his role of coach, they saw a tremendous example of servant leadership. It was as if listening to the ugliness of their challenges and helping them discover their own plans for action was equivalent to washing their feet. They thought, *What a brilliant spiritual leader Phil is! And what an example of faith he is for us, trusting that God will provide the answers for each of our unique situations.*

Eventually, Phil took a hard look at one of his favorite parts of his role as pastor–preaching. He was convinced coaching helps people realize their full Kingdom potential. In that light, he thought, since preaching was the one time each week when he had the greatest opportunity to inspire his congregation through God's Word, he might be able to incorporate a coach approach into his preaching. For him, that meant asking more discovery questions in his preaching. Whether they were actually answered aloud by the congregation or not didn't matter to Phil. The brain process of connecting the dots for greater learning would still be happening. It also meant focusing more on facilitating the congregation to design actions for themselves as a result of each sermon that he preached. He had fun telling the congregation that he no longer wanted to hear, "Good sermon, pastor," on the front steps as they exited. From now on, he wanted to hear, "Here's what my action is going to be this week."

Somewhere along the way Phil realized that he had to let go of having to have all the answers. What a freeing experience! Now more than ever before in his ministry, he realized that God was really the one in charge. It was exciting to see how God was working in the lives of the people. Phil was just glad to be a part of it.

Can You Coach Others?

Since you have benefited from *Christ-Centered* coaching, you might be able to coach others. Some of the basic skills that *Christ-Centered* coaches use are the same as skills needed to be an effective ministry leader: intensive listening, discovery questions, and direct communication.

My way of describing people who were born to coach is to say, "They have the blood type C–for coach." So how do you know if you have the blood type C? Ask yourself these questions and give an objective answer. If you answer in the affirmative to many of them, you might be a natural coach.

1. I have been listening intently, asking discovery questions, and encouraging others as a preferred way of interacting with people all my life.
2. I always respond this way (as in question 1). It extends beyond work life. I often do it in addition to my current job, sometimes even instead of performing well in my current job.
3. I can see the benefit of and enjoy having structured conversations so others will take effective intentional action.
4. I am inclined to make fine distinctions in language to clarify meaning.
5. I naturally put my own agenda aside in deference to the person with whom I'm talking.
6. I naturally see patterns in behavior that others don't see.
7. I recognize and can share trends that result in others being more effective.
8. I naturally value and prefer to invest in people and relationships rather than in equipment, tasks, or projects.
9. I have a keen awareness for underlying strengths, for what is not said, and for possibilities that are not yet realized.
10. I have a natural fascination with human interaction and am a student of human behavior (this might include reading, seminars, etc., and is not limited to formal education or degrees).

Benefits of Coaching

Coaching Others		God-Sized Goals	
Intentional Progress			
Clarity/Focus	Confidence		Learning
Orienting around Strengths			

You Don't Have to Have All the Answers

Do you really have all the answers? Is that even possible? What a burden that places on any ministry leader! *Christ-Centered* coaching of others frees you from having to know it all.

Letting go of having to have all the answers is a freeing experience. Ministry leaders who have themselves been coached and then go on to coach other leaders in their church or ministry often talk about the lifting of a huge burden. They no longer have to provide guidance on every topic for every leader. Having that burden lifted allows them to spend more of their efforts on the things they were gifted and called to do.

Having to deal with the expectations of others is a reality for all ministry leaders. If the people you lead expect answers and you suddenly start asking questions, they may wonder what is going on and begin to mistrust you as a leader. Because your approach has changed, those who work with you may feel they can no longer anticipate how you will respond.

To ensure continuing positive relationships, before you start firing the questions in a coaching mode, you need to explain your interest in using a coaching style. Tell your leaders why you want to change your behavior to ask questions. Explain the benefits you have experienced from being coached, and let them know that you want them to benefit as you have from your experience. Sharing from your own experience is a powerful way to compel them to think of your leadership in a different way and opens them up to being willing to discover their own answers.

Christ-Centered coaching others allows people to surpass you. That might be a scary thought if you receive your value from having to do more, know more, achieve more than those with whom you work. But allowing others to surpass you is another way of measuring success. It's actually a way to leave an even greater legacy—especially in Kingdom work—to know that those you've coached will have better ideas, to have greater success, to have a broader impact. Knowing that you have helped others have the resources not only to achieve but to keep on succeeding because they can meet needs as they evolve is rewarding in itself. It's a perfect plan for people who are energized by results instead of acclaim.

The biblical models are many. Barnabas, the encourager, was listed first until he and Paul began their first missionary journey together. After that, Paul took the lead, and Barnabas slipped into the background.

It's a lot like being meek, seeing the last be first and the first be last. It's a lot like Jesus saying, "The one who believes in me will also do the works that I do and, in fact, will do greater works than these, because I am going to the Father" (John 14:12).

It's a lot like loving your neighbor and loving God with all your strength.

The truth is, great coaches don't just allow those they coach to surpass them; they work toward it. They are most gratified when it happens.

What a blessing it is to have everyone you lead in your ministry thriving and doing more than you could ever imagine doing yourself. Now that's full Kingdom potential!

Christ-Centered Coaching Is a Tool for Multiplying Efforts

Let's return to Phil's story. Remember, Phil is fictitious and represents several ministry leaders that I've coached, but they, collectively, went through a similar process.

When I first started coaching Phil, Phil was the gatekeeper for progress in his church. If Phil was present or participating in something, it was making progress. If Phil didn't at least publicly affirm a program or ministry, it was doomed to failure or at least struggled to survive.

As the church continued to grow, Phil soon realized that he couldn't be everywhere at once. But, in spite of physical limitations, he felt compelled to stay involved in every team because of a subconscious realization that progress was only happening in the areas where he was personally giving his attention.

Phil's family was not pleased. The faster the church grew, the less time they had with their husband and father. When Phil started coaching ministry team leaders, they discovered next steps for themselves and designed their own action steps to be taken outside of the actual conversation with Phil. While the ministry team leader was taking action, Phil was at home with his family.

Note that Phil began with a ministry team leader he already had a good relationship with, one who was doing his work well. He didn't begin with the person in the church who gave him the most problems, the person he thought most needed to be "fixed." He chose someone who wanted to reach full Kingdom potential, who was already trying to do his best and to grow. Note that this also follows Jesus' example. With one notable exception, Jesus chose men who would learn from him and establish his church after he was gone from them. The men were radically different from one another, but they had one thing in common: they followed the Master, sat at his feet to hear question after question and parable after parable, learned from him, and followed his example. Because of what they did in leading people to

Christ and establishing the church, we, too, have the privilege of knowing Jesus Christ as Savior and following their example in telling others.

The more Phil coached ministry team leaders, the more progress began happening in multiple areas of the church all at once. Phil's time spent coaching was much smaller in comparison to the amount of time he had spent directing all the church's ministries. After he began coaching, where was Phil while the progress was happening? He was at home getting refueled or doing the other parts of his ministry that had been neglected. He was spending more quiet time with the Lord. He was spending more time in his study on sermon preparation. And he had more time for caregiving and building relationships instead of programs.

Was Phil any less involved in forward progress? Not really. He had had a hand in much of what was happening because of his role as coach. But he had not been the one who supplied the answers. Since he did not supply the answers, the ministry team leaders were not codependent on him to make progress. The result of this was more like "equipping the saints," because he was getting them to be fully engaged in the process and able to act independently from his direction.

Each of the people like Phil whom I have coached were surprised at one of the responses they received from those they coached. Consistently, people coached by ministry leaders talk about how their walk with the Lord improved. They had drawn closer to God in Bible study or taken bigger steps of faith or understood better how they could serve. They felt more alive in their faith and more engaged in living their faith. They felt that they finally understood how they were fulfilling God's purpose, the divine call on their lives. Isn't that what ministry leaders are after in the first place?

Those who love the Lord with *all* their strength inspire others to love the Lord with all *their* strength.

Christ-Centered Coaching Is Servant Leadership
Christ-Centered coaching is serving.

To do an effective job of coaching others, *Christ-Centered* coaches have to put aside their own agenda and help those being coached to achieve their agenda. Coaches have to care as much about others' success as their own. Coaches have to be there when others fail to help pick them up and head them in the direction of progress.

Coaching is about others' strengths. It's about *their* clarity and focus, *their* addressing their fears, and *their* determining what needs to be learned. It's not about you/the coach/the ministry leader and your knowledge of Scripture or your experience in ministry or your connection to God. It's all about *theirs.*

Christ-Centered coaching is leading.

This concept is more of a stretch for ministry leaders to accept at first, until they try it. In working with many leaders in both ministry and business, I've noticed a pattern of behavior present in the leaders who are the most successful at leading. Leaders who focus on having followers tend to lose the focus on developing their own leadership skills and start to focus only on the followers and their ability to follow. Inevitably, with this focus, the leaders determine that the real issue is that they don't have people who know how to follow.

But leaders who focus on developing leaders who can develop leaders are more successful at honing their own leadership skills. It is a phenomenon akin to understanding content better when you teach it to someone else. Coaching is a leadership tool in that respect; it helps you develop others as leaders.

If you define *leadership* as "influencing others to live their full Kingdom potential," coaching is a very effective leadership tool.[1]

Christ-Centered Coaching Equips for Evangelism and Discipleship

The Great Commission tells us to make disciples of all nations. Coaching helps equip disciples to do this.

When I am coaching business leaders, a distinct pattern spans varying amounts of time for each person. The pattern goes something like this: They first come to coaching sessions with a challenge, often needing to decide between a good choice and a bad choice. We use their definitions of good and bad. The challenges will point to the underlying source of not orienting around strengths, lack of clarity and focus, fears that have not been successfully addressed, and not having an effective plan for continued learning. As we address those, they start making intentional progress.

At that point, the challenges shift to making choices between multiple good things. At this point I suggest that the way to choose between good and good is to look to their values and beliefs for guidance.

While I've seen this pattern over and over, one time was particularly poignant. I was coaching a senior executive of a very large corporation. When I asked him to go to his values and beliefs for guidance, he paused for what seemed like forever and then said, "I don't think that I have any of those. Yours seem to work for you, so why don't you tell me what yours are, and I'll just adopt them."

After I picked myself up off the floor (it was a phone coaching session), I said I'd be glad to share my values and beliefs with him but that one's worldview is very personal and that each person has to make choices on this topic. Being a coach, I'm not interested in telling but in prompting discovery; at his insistence I did share with him my values and beliefs.

When I had finished, he said, "Sounds like something I would like to adopt." After several months of having him discover what it would mean to apply belief in Jesus Christ as Savior to his decision-making processes, he said, "I know this might be highly unusual, but would you mind sharing this information with my wife as well? She's seeing the difference in me and is asking questions that I can't answer since I'm new at this."

The process of coaching this executive and the place that he took the conversation, at his own pace and with direct application to the decisions he was making on a daily basis, was a much easier process of evangelism for me than The Four Spiritual Laws had ever been. This experience and many more like it in my executive coaching eventually caused me to start working with ministry leaders on the topic of coaching. I felt compelled to tell the church what a great tool coaching is for introducing nonbelievers to Jesus Christ so that they can learn what loving the Lord and servant leadership are about by allowing them to experience it. And it works consistently.

Such experiences have caused me to develop a large vision. It is my dream that one day, when people in the workplace have challenges, they will say, "I need a coach." That's what I'm working toward in my corporate coaching efforts. And the very next thought that comes to their minds will be, *Where's a Christian? Christians are great coaches.* That's what I'm working toward when I coach ministry leaders. Making this vision a reality will probably take longer than my lifetime, and many ministry leaders will need to learn how to use coaching in their ministries to make it happen.

Being coached and experiencing these benefits, including having the *Christ-Centered* coaching you have received rubbing off on others, will aid in this dream's becoming a reality. Let me just thank you in advance for joining me in this journey. By the way, guess where my vision was created–in a coaching session!

Biblical Connection
Jesus set the ultimate example for servant leadership.
John 13 pictures it beautifully:

> After he had washed their feet, had put on his robe, and had returned to the table, he said to them, "Do you know what I have done to you? You call me Teacher and Lord—and you are right, for that is what I am. So if I, your Lord and Teacher, have washed your feet, you also ought to wash one another's feet. For I have set you an example, that you also should do as I have done to you. Very truly, I tell you, servants are not greater than their master, nor are messengers greater than the one who sent them. If you know these things, you are blessed if you do them." (John 13:12–17)

Jesus' example just before his crucifixion was consistent with what he had been teaching the disciples all along:

> "Blessed are the meek, for they will inherit the earth." (Matthew 5:5)

> "But many who are first will be last, and the last will be first." (Mark 10:31)

> "'You shall love the Lord your God with all your heart, and with all your soul, and with all your mind, and with all your strength.' The second is this, 'You shall love your neighbor as yourself.'" (Mark 12:30–31)

Paul continued the theme of servant leadership:

> The gifts he gave were…to equip the saints for the work of ministry, for building up the body of Christ, until all of us come to the unity of the faith and of the knowledge of the Son of God, to maturity, to the measure of the full stature of Christ. (Ephesians 4:11–13)

Tips for *Christ-Centered* Coaches
- If you spot ministry leaders with the blood type C, tell them what you see as strengths in them and then coach them to discover what they might do with that information.
- A positive correlation exists between blood type C and how coachable a person is. In other words, most coaches are highly coachable. A coach who is not highly coachable would raise a red flag.

Tips for Working with a *Christ-Centered* Coach

- If you have blood type C, you might want to pursue being more intentional in coaching others to reach their full Kingdom potential. Get coach training.[2] There's much more to masterful coaching than meets the eye. In fact, the better your coach is, the more your conversations will feel like a chat with a trusted friend and may cause you erroneously to think the process is easily executed.
- If you don't have blood type C, you can still incorporate more of a coach approach than you currently are for the purpose of helping others move forward. Some coach training will help here as well.

CHAPTER 10

Christ-Centered Coaching Encourages God-Sized Goals

Now to him who by the power at work within us is able to accomplish abundantly far more than all we can ask or imagine, to him be glory in the church and in Christ Jesus to all generations, forever and ever.

EPHESIANS 3:20–21

Stephanie was a denominational leader. For many years she served in the area of women's ministry. She loved her work and was good at it. Her work was going well, with no real challenges. When she heard a friend in another area of denominational ministry talk about using a coach, she became curious. Usually an early adopter of new ideas, Stephanie was always interested in maximizing her potential, so the idea of coaching really intrigued her.

After interviewing three different Christian coaches, each of whom seemed competent but with different styles, she picked the one that she simply felt more at home with and scheduled her first two coaching sessions. Even this part of the process had been interesting for Stephanie. Who could have imagined she would have a choice among so many Christian coaches? Who would have guessed that their approaches would differ so much? The first coach she talked with gave her good advice when she insisted that she interview at least three.

Her new coach sent her a covenant document that explained what coaching is, what she could expect from her coach, and what would be expected of her. Hearing her coach describe the typical process, what to expect, and what is expected helped Stephanie begin to think about the process and to realize this was a commitment that would require work.

She and her coach spent the first session just getting to know each other. Stephanie shared more of her background than she had in the interview. Her coach shared more about how the coaching process would work and some of the benefits she could expect to gain from the coaching experience. The coach asked Stephanie to talk about her vision for the future and her short- and long-term goals for her ministry.

Stephanie mentioned wanting to take her ministry to new heights to impact more women nationwide and to have a more lasting impact on their lives. The coach was excited. Stephanie was going to be coachable. She didn't come to coaching to whine but to maximize her Kingdom potential. The coach already knew Stephanie would quickly benefit from the process and expand her ministry. Because the coach had been there before, she was already looking forward to the God-sized goals Stephanie would accomplish.

Stephanie felt burdened that she didn't see leaders emerging from the younger women, so she wanted to focus there. Her coach said, "Since you want to make a nationwide impact and grow leaders, what would that actually look like?"

Stephanie would need time to think about that because nothing she wasn't already doing came to mind immediately. She thought that it was a good question, but when she looked at the clock, she saw that the session was nearly over. She thought that might be best. That would give her time to talk to some of the other women's ministry leaders and to pray about what God wanted her to do to reach young women to lead in this ministry.

This was consistent with the covenant Stephanie had signed. She knew that she would be expected to take some kind of action as a result of every session. The actions could range from making a shift in her thinking and realigning her future actions to that shift, to having a much-needed conversation with someone to move the relationship forward, to developing new goals and plans. A myriad of other options for action were also possible.

Stephanie decided that her action between these first two sessions would be to think about what a nationwide impact would look like and write it down. She knew that if she wrote it down, it would take better shape and would have more detail than if she just kept wondering about it. The truth was, she'd been thinking about this very idea a lot. She just needed this discipline to begin putting details to her vision.

When asked what might have been an "aha" experience for her in this first session, Stephanie replied, "I've been saying that I wanted to take my ministry to a new level and have nationwide impact for a couple of years now. But I was surprised that I had never really thought about what form such an impact would take. I'm almost ashamed to say that out loud."

At the end of the coaching session, Stephanie felt that, if nothing else, she could see the value of having someone else prompt her and ask these probing questions that might push her into gear on dreams she'd always put off. This was going to be good.

The next session was two weeks away. That would give her plenty of time to "do her homework," to write up her plans, or so she thought.

The first week was a zoo. With a regional conference coming up on the weekend, she had to deal with all the last-minute details from programs to changes in housing arrangements for one of the guest speakers to finding a substitute for a breakout speaker whose youngest child had gotten sick. Somehow no homework was done, and only a week remained before the next session.

While she was busy getting ready for the conference, all her other work piled up. She needed to return phone calls and review publications. Where would she have time to think about her nationwide initiative? She needed substantial quiet time if she was going to do this right.

Two days before the next coaching session, Stephanie realized that she didn't have anything written down. In fact, she hadn't been able to give the topic any thought at all. And this weekend was going to be full with her son's band competition all day Saturday and her normal responsibilities in her own church on Sunday. It just wasn't going to happen. She was beginning to wonder whether coaching was a good idea after all. No wonder she had never launched her nationwide plan. She could hardly keep up with what she already had to do. She had begun this process with great intentions, but now she wasn't so sure.

She called her coach. "I'm so sorry that I haven't done my homework for our session. I had the best intentions, but it just didn't get done. I'll spare you all the details, but it's not like I was just sitting around doing nothing for the last two weeks. Can we reschedule?"

Her coach responded, "Thanks for calling, but let's not reschedule. Come to the call Monday, and we'll talk about the barriers that prevented you from doing the homework, and maybe we can do some brainstorming together about what your nationwide impact would look like. How's that?"

Stephanie's situation is not unique. The coach knew that Stephanie already had her plate full, but she also knew that getting the most from a coaching relationship means dealing with the barriers, making the commitment to make the "homework" a priority. Her coach explained that rescheduling usually tends to add to a person's frustration, while talking through the barriers gives motivation to accomplish the desired action. Rescheduling is like breaking a promise to yourself, only now you've exacerbated the situation by also breaking a covenant you've signed and a verbal commitment that you've made to your coach. For some that first rescheduling could lead to a downward spiral of excuses and self-blame. But keeping the scheduled meeting can reenergize the process and lead to a positive upward spiral of productivity.

In a way Stephanie was glad the coach didn't let her delay their meeting. She really wanted to do this, and she felt good that when the meeting began her coach would already know that she had not completed the action she'd agreed to take. That took some pressure off, and she looked forward to their conversation on Monday. She responded to the coach, "Sounds good. I feel bad that I didn't do what I said I would do. Thanks for understanding. I'll call you on Monday."

The coach, already concerned about Stephanie and building a relationship with her, replied, "Great. I hope your son's band wins!"

On Monday the session started with Stephanie giving an update of the wonderful craziness of the last two weeks. Her coach asked, "What would be most helpful for us to talk about today?"

Stephanie answered, "I really do want to write down a plan for that nationwide impact. Frankly, all my weeks are full of activity just like the last two. Could we spend this time helping me get started on this?"

"Sure. Let me start this from another angle. Think of a ministry that you would say is having a nationwide impact already. What are the characteristics that make it successful?" The coach guessed that part of Stephanie's problem wasn't just lack of time but the need for a fresh perspective to help her think in new ways about her vision.

"I know someone who is known nationwide for doing workplace ministry. Is that what you mean?"

"Sure. What are the characteristics that make her ministry successful?"

"One thing I like is the newsletter she does. It goes out to thousands of people once a week. She also has training that she does in churches and at conference centers about how to start a workplace ministry in local churches. Lots of folks go there to learn, and then some of them do some additional training to be able to train others. Last year she started teaching her courses in a seminary, and people can now get a Master of Divinity in special ministries focused on workplace ministry. Her newsletter last week said that other seminaries now want the same curriculum. She asked her readers to pray that that would be successfully negotiated. She's also written a book that's coming out next month, and I'm looking forward to reading it."

"Wow, that's a lot. You really know a lot about this person." The coach continued to nudge Stephanie to analyze what she liked in the other woman's approach to ministry.

"Yes, I'm inspired that she has done so many innovative things and is having such an impact."

"What would you have to do to have that kind of impact?" The coach turned from information to application.

"Oh, I don't think I could do all that. In fact, I can list all the reasons that I couldn't do what she does. For one, I'm not a writer. But more than that, I don't know as many people as she does."

"We can deal with how to overcome barriers before you actually take any actions. For now let's just figure out what would have to be done for your ministry to have such an impact." The coach doesn't accept the barriers because she believes Stephanie is well on her way to the excitement of getting involved in something only God can do. The coach sees the barriers as keeping her from achieving her God-given vision, her God-sized goal. The coach knows that God is not the source of barriers, so the coach wants to help Stephanie focus on the possibilities rather than the reason the dream can't happen.

Stephanie replied with honest conviction: "You know, I'm having a bit of trouble with this conversation. First, I don't think I have what it takes to do something that big. But beyond that, where's God in all of this? I don't think I would want to get ahead of what God's plan is in all of this. And just looking at someone else's ministry to figure out what I could replicate doesn't seem right either. I'm not sure what to do next. I think I'm more confused now than I was when we first started talking."

Stephanie's response was not unusual, so her coach was ready to respond: "I'm guessing this is not the first time you've faced a dilemma like this in your ministry. When you find yourself in this type spot, how do you deal with it?"

"I haven't often felt that I was in such a situation, but I do recall a couple of times when I faced making a huge decision that would affect the direction of my life. I set aside extra time for prayer and Bible study and tried to spend more time listening to the Lord."

"Would this be a time that you would want to do that again?"

"Yes, I think that would be a great idea. I'm calming down. I was getting nervous about embarking on something larger than I can handle. I have had times before that I came up with a 'brilliant' plan for my ministry and God was nowhere in it. I really don't want to repeat that. I felt that was where the conversation was going, and it made me feel uncomfortable. Slowing down to listen more to God at this point is what I need."

"Good. So what are you specifically going to do and when will you do it?"

Stephanie responded, "You just don't let up, do you?"

"Well, after all, we do have to get to action for this to be a coaching session."

In subsequent coaching sessions, Stephanie identified some creative actions to take. She interviewed the person she admired who was doing the nationwide workplace ministry. She learned that there was software to create newsletters that made it easier to create one than she had thought. And she thought she'd give it a try—on a quarterly basis to start. She identified five young women who showed leadership potential that she would like to invest in to help develop their leadership abilities. She also decided that she would develop a breakout session for her own conference next year on the latest innovations in women's ministries to try her hand at reaching a younger audience.

Over the next year she was amazed at how much of her dream to have nationwide impact was becoming reality and how solid she felt that she was right in the middle of what God was calling her to do and be. Things had not happened as she had anticipated, but it was a fun adventure to see what would develop next. She just stayed focused on one step at a time and in taking actions toward her goals instead of just expecting them to happen without her participation. She was learning once again to depend on God each step of the way.

Just recently she received a call from a ministry leader in another country asking if she could help them begin women's ministries there. Stephanie was thrilled. Her vision was nationwide, but God's plan was worldwide. More than amazing!

Providing Support for God-Sized Goals

Coaching provides support for God-sized goals—those opportunities that go beyond what we know how to do or know we can control. *Christ-Centered* coaches frequently get to enjoy seeing people reach this level, seeing God work in amazing ways.

I was reintroduced to this concept several years ago when a dear friend and coaching colleague of mine, Linda Miller, and I decided to study the books *Experiencing God*[1] and *If You Want to Walk on Water, You've Got to Get out of the Boat.*[2] We had a special time of reading these books for application in our own lives and also looking at them in light of how we could better coach people on this topic. As with many things in my life, once I started focusing on this topic in my own life, it started showing up in coaching conversations. I've found it to be one of the more privileged experiences of my life to watch someone embark on God-sized goals—and achieve them!

Benefits of Coaching

Coaching Others		God-Sized Goals	
Intentional Progress			
Clarity/Focus	Confidence		Learning
Orienting around Strengths			

When coaches work with secular people, often these people are, for the first time, doing what they were created to do, and they are finding great joy in their work. But they don't realize God's hand in creating them with a unique set of strengths and abilities that are a perfect fit for God's plan for their life. *Christ-Centered* coaches especially enjoy getting to share these moments with fellow Christians who find this joy and at the same time know that they can only thank God for bringing this to fruition.

Not everyone reaches this level. Many people embark on this path, but not everyone finishes the journey. It's not an easy road. Having a *Christ-Centered* coach can help infuse the process with courage to keep you going, to encourage you to keep searching for God's instructions and keep taking the actions that would keep you on the God-sized path.

Even though the path may not be easy, it is worth pursuing because it affirms that God is in control of your life and ministry.

When you truly embark on God-sized goals, there is no mistaking that God is the one who deserves the glory.

A different level of joy and resilience results. Because you are so aware of God's leading you one step at a time, you will find greater ability to deal with day-by-day routine frustrations. The dependence that is essential when taking on a God-sized goal creates a positive, upward spiral that generates enthusiasm and vision for even greater Kingdom goals.

How *Christ-Centered* Coaching Helps

The Bible tells the story of people who stepped up to God-sized goals:

• Abraham left home not knowing where God was taking him.
• Moses led his people out of slavery even though at first he didn't have the confidence to speak to Pharaoh.
• Mary chose to give birth to God's Son.
• The disciples left their professions, followed Jesus, and started the Christian church movement.
• Paul made an about-face from persecuting Christians to taking the good news to distant places.

What did these and many others have in common, and how does coaching facilitate these experiences?

They were originally headed in a different direction.

Initially Stephanie was focused on developing younger leaders. During the coaching sessions she realized that she had even bigger goals, but she was too intimidated to act on them. By working with a coach, she was able to address her fears and take actions on both fronts.

No one made a bigger turnaround than Paul. On the road to Damascus, en route to kill Christians, God stopped him in his tracks and changed his life from persecuting Christians to multiplying them.

They felt inadequate for the task.

People who reach this level of *Christ-Centered* coaching benefits typically feel inadequate for a huge task. Perhaps they feel like Isaiah did: "Woe is me! I am lost, for I am a man of unclean lips, and I live among a people of unclean lips; yet my eyes have seen the King, the LORD of hosts!" (Isaiah 6:5). Maybe they lack faith in themselves; maybe they don't have enough faith in God. Either way, this situation is not intimidating to a *Christ-Centered* coach because the coach knows that it is good for ministry leaders to need to depend totally on God instead of themselves.

A *Christ-Centered* coach helps you address your fears instead of avoiding them. A coach will also get you to identify the strengths you can leverage instead of focusing on all the things that you can and can't do. Additionally, a coach will have you identify the things that you need to learn to bridge gaps in your knowledge.

They acknowledged God as Lord of their lives.

Not all who call Jesus Savior make him Lord of their lives. Stephanie had long ago put God first in her life. She knew that she had to go to her source of strength and power. Without that acknowledgment that God is in control, we could do nothing. John 15:5 had proved true in her life over and over again: "I am the vine, you are the branches. Those who abide in me and I in them bear much fruit, because apart from me you can do nothing."

A *Christ-Centered* coach can help you stay grounded in your relationship with God so that you can continue to tap into the power that is available to you in Jesus Christ. Maintaining your relationship with Christ requires action too. What those actions ought to be are valid topics for discussion with your *Christ-Centered* coach.

They made a choice to follow.

This is what Isaiah did: "Then I heard the voice of the Lord saying, 'Whom shall I send, and who will go for us?' And I said, 'Here am I; send me!'" (Isaiah 6:8).

Following Christ is a choice. It was for the first disciples. It is for Christians today. That choice is an action. James has a lot to say about a Christian's responsibility to continue taking action:

> But be doers of the word, and not merely hearers who deceive themselves. (James 1:22)

> You see that faith was active along with his works, and faith was brought to completion by the works. (James 2:22)

> Submit yourselves therefore to God. Resist the devil, and he will flee from you. Draw near to God, and he will draw near to you. Cleanse your hands, you sinners, and purify your hearts, you double-minded. Lament and mourn and weep. Let your laughter be turned into mourning and your joy into dejection. Humble yourselves before the Lord, and he will exalt you. (James 4:7–10)

All Christians take actions. Simply choosing not to choose *is* a choice. Paul often talks about making actions consistent with the choice made to follow Christ. A *Christ-Centered* coach will encourage you to be intentional in your progress. In some ways you can think of Paul as the first Christian coach. Most coaching is done on the phone. Paul didn't have the luxury of such technology. Because he didn't, he did his coaching through the letters he wrote, and so we can continue to learn from his words today. He didn't have to be face-to-face to help people discover how to live a life consistent with the commitment they made to follow Christ. True, Paul did a lot of telling. But now that you know more about coaching, look closely at Paul's words, and you'll see that he also did a lot of "drawing out."

Difficulties don't go away as a result of the choice; they may even increase.

For Paul, things went from bad to worse. He went from being the persecutor to being persecuted. But he said that his suffering was worth it:

> "I did not shrink from doing anything helpful, proclaiming the message to you and teaching you publicly and from house to house, as I testified to both Jews and Greeks about repentance toward God and faith toward our Lord Jesus. And now, as a captive to the Spirit, I am on my way to Jerusalem, not knowing what will happen to me there, except that the Holy Spirit testifies to me in every city that imprisonment and persecutions are waiting for me. But I do not count my life of any value to myself, if only I may finish my course and the ministry that I received from the Lord Jesus, to testify to the good news of God's grace." (Acts 20:20–24)

To be involved in God-sized goals requires perseverance. The Letter to the Hebrews is a great book of encouragement. The writer wrote: "Do not, therefore, abandon that confidence of yours; it brings a great reward. For you need endurance, so that when you have done the will of God, you may receive what was promised" (Hebrews 10:35–36).

A *Christ-Centered* coach offers you a safe place for discussing all the ups and downs of your journey so that you can stay on the path to the calling that God has set before you. With a coach you can talk about your challenges, the barriers thrown in your way, your doubts and fears, the things that distract you, your weariness, and also your joy!

Their results inspire our faith today.

Hebrews 11, the roll call of the faithful, records some of the names of those who glorified God by being involved in something they could not have done by their own power alone but that God had done through them. The same would be true of you. A coach will be your best advocate, in some cases believing in you before you believe in yourself.

You may be thinking that these biblical heroes didn't have a coach, so why do you need one today? While the people mentioned may not have had a coach the way we'd define that role, they did have support. Paul had Barnabas. Elizabeth had Mary. Moses had Aaron and Jethro. Life in community is a significant theme in both the Hebrew Bible and the New Testament. "One another" passages are scattered throughout the books of the Bible; working with a *Christ-Centered* coach is a great way to live out these instructions.

Paul wrote about the interconnectedness of the body of Christ. Each member is uniquely gifted. *Christ-Centered* coaches, members of the body of Christ, have gifts to enable others to find and fulfill their God-given purpose. "But strive for the greater gifts. And I will show you a still more excellent way. If I speak in the tongues of mortals and of angels, but do not have love, I am a noisy gong or a clanging cymbal" (1 Corinthians 12:31–13:1).

Showing love is an action. Isn't this what Jesus taught? He commanded us to love one another. "This is my commandment, that you love one another as I have loved you. No one has greater love than this, to lay down one's life for one's friends" (John 15:12–13). Loving God with all your strength means putting love into action, in obedience to Christ. The role of a *Christ-Centered* coach is to prompt people to Christian action.

God intended for us to live in community, to love one another, to be priests to one another, and to call one another to accountability for our actions before God. Those who have the gifts to coach are uniquely equipped to help others in this role. Christians, the body of Christ, should call out those gifts and use them to build the Kingdom.

Embarking on a God-Sized Goal

Embarking on a God-sized goal will comprise several things:

- Involve building on the momentum of your intentional progress. Other benefits have to happen to get to this point.
- Challenge you beyond your comfort zone. Don't confuse going beyond your comfort zone with going beyond the realm of your

strengths. Going beyond your comfort zone is a valid way to stretch yourself and to take a step of faith with God in charge.

- Involve a dynamic adventure for yourself and those around you. It's a great way to put faith into action and in doing so to witness to others. When people see you taking on a God-sized goal and living in faith one day at a time, when they see your positive energy as you reach your full Kingdom potential, they will want what you have. And you'll have opportunity to tell them the reason for your hope. Peter wrote:

> Now who will harm you if you are eager to do what is good? But even if you do suffer for doing what is right, you are blessed. Do not fear what they fear, and do not be intimidated, but in your hearts sanctify Christ as Lord. Always be ready to make your defense to anyone who demands from you an accounting for the hope that is in you. (1 Peter 3:13–15)

Produce joy in your life. Knowing that you are doing what God intended you to do leads to contentment above all else. Jesus called his followers to rest in him and then put on a yoke. That means work, action. But resting in him assures that the yoke is a perfect fit.

> "Come to me, all you that are weary and are carrying heavy burdens, and I will give you rest. Take my yoke upon you, and learn from me; for I am gentle and humble in heart, and you will find rest for your souls. For my yoke is easy, and my burden is light." (Matthew 11:28–30)

All Your Strength Benefits

What did you notice about the coach in each of the scenarios?

- The coach listened intently, loved unconditionally.
- The coach asked lots of questions, not to interrogate but to help the person being coached to think deeply.
- The coach didn't give the answers, knowing that the best answers for the person being coached would come from that person.
- The coach supported the person being coached with encouragement and partnership, a coming alongside that is totally focused on the individual's having the freedom to thrive.
- The coach inspired the one being coached on at least one if not more of these:
  - ~ to know their strengths
  - ~ to be clear and focused
  - ~ to address fears instead of avoiding them

~ to keep going and to continue learning
~ to move forward intentionally
~ to step up to the adventure of a God-sized calling

What would it mean for you to love the Lord with *all* your strength?

- You'd have to know your strengths. Some you may have known about for years, but others probably lie hidden.
- You'd have to know what *all* would mean for you. Since everyone has some untapped potential, this will be a lifelong journey.
- You'd have to identify the actions you need to take that would be considered "loving the Lord."

What are the gaps between where you are now in your ministry and what loving with *all* your strength would look like? What could your ministry be like with the kind of support that comes from this kind of coaching? Just imagine.

Words from the Word

The Bible says that we can do more than we think we can through Christ Jesus our Lord:

> Now to him who by the power at work within us is able to accomplish abundantly far more than all we can ask or imagine, to him be glory in the church and in Christ Jesus to all generations, forever and ever. (Ephesians 3:20–21)

Jesus said that he must go away in order for the Holy Spirit, the paraclete, the one who comes alongside to come:

> "It is to your advantage that I go away, for if I do not go away, the Advocate will not come to you; but if I go, I will send him to you." (John 16:7)

A *Christ-Centered* coach is also one who comes alongside you.

Jesus said that when he went away, his followers would do even greater things:

> "The one who believes in me will also do the works that I do and, in fact, will do greater works than these." (John 14:12)

This is a great model for *Christ-Centered* coaches who also expect those they coach to surpass them. In this way coaching does not have the limitations of mentoring and consulting, which tend to train people to become like an expert. Coaching helps you become all that you can become.

While most of the book has been spent talking about loving the Lord with all of your strength, let's look back at the Great Commandment. We've touched on all of these points. *Love the Lord your God with all your heart*–choose to live **with intentional progress** (chapter 8) toward yielding fully to **God-sized goals** (chapter 10)–*and with all your soul*–live, with **clarity and focus,** the purpose God created you for (chapter 5)–*and with all your mind*–use the brain God gave you for **learning** continuously (chapter 7)–*and with all your strength*–orient your life around the **strengths** that you were born with (chapter 4) and realize your full Kingdom potential (the whole book). *Love your neighbor as yourself*–receive encouragement and unconditional love, which will build your own **confidence,** then share that encouragement and love with others (chapter 6). All of the parts of the Great Commandment are connected to benefits that come from being coached. And when you **coach others** (chapter 9), you facilitate others in living the Great Commandment as well.

Tips for *Christ-Centered* Coaches

- If you think you could only do coaching in person, try the phone. As long as you make sure there are no visual distractions, your listening will most likely be heightened because your brain can be dedicated to what it is hearing and not be distracted by what it is seeing. Not being able to see nonverbal cues will not be as much of a deficit as you might think.
- If you think that you can only do coaching on the phone, try coaching in person. Nothing replaces your physical presence as encouragement and support. It's really hard–but not impossible– to give a hug over the phone.
- The best arrangement? If possible, schedule a mixture of in-person sessions and phone sessions. It's the best of both worlds.

Tips for Working with a *Christ-Centered* Coach

- Don't skip coaching sessions just because you are not prepared, especially early on in the coaching relationship. Your coach can help you overcome the barriers and develop the habit of coming prepared.
- If you must miss a session, be considerate and call with as much notice as possible to reschedule. The last thing you want to do is have your coach waiting for a call that does not happen.
- Be ready to stretch! Before you know it, you will be soaring.

Prayers of a
Christ-Centered Coach

Lord, thank you for calling me to be a coach.
- Let your unconditional love flow through me.
- Spotlight my sins that encumber.
- Mold me into a servant leader.

Before each coaching conversation, I pray
- for boldness to be your ambassador
- for the ones I'm coaching to listen to you
- for your direction, insights, and inspiration to take action

During each coaching conversation, I pray
- for guidance from you on what to say and how to say it
- for wisdom to know when to turn the conversation into a time of prayer
- for peace when it is time to be silent and let you do all the speaking

And beyond each coaching conversation, I pray
- for fears of the unknown to be calmed
- for you to fill in the gaps of what was not said and what was really needed beyond the surface
- for boldness to take actions that go beyond what we know how to do and outcomes we know we can control
- for followers of you, Lord, and not followers of the coach
- for Christian coaches and their global impact
- for coaches everywhere who are making the ground fertile for the gospel

May *you* be the one who is glorified in all we say and do.
In Jesus' name, *Amen.*

JANE CRESWELL

APPENDIX 1

The ICF Philosophy of Coaching

The International Coach Federation adheres to a form of coaching that honors the client as the expert in his/her life and work, and believes that every client is creative, resourceful, and whole. Standing on this foundation, the coach's responsibility is to:

- Discover, clarify, and align with what the client wants to achieve;
- Encourage client self-discovery;
- Elicit client-generated solutions and strategies;
- Hold the client responsible and accountable.

Overview of Coaching Competencies

A. Setting the Foundation
    1. Meeting Ethical Guidelines and Professional Standards
    2. Establishing the Coaching Agreement
B. Co-creating the Relationship
    3. Establishing Trust and Intimacy with the Client
    4. Coaching Presence
C. Communicating Effectively
    5. Active Listening
    6. Powerful Questioning
    7. Direct Communication
D. Facilitating Learning and Results
    8. Creating Awareness
    9. Designing Actions
    10. Planning and Goal Setting
    11. Managing Progress and Accountability

The ICF Standards of Ethical Conduct

Professional Conduct at Large

As a coach:

1. I will conduct myself in a manner that reflects positively upon the coaching profession, and I will refrain from engaging in conduct or making statements that may negatively impact the public's understanding or acceptance of coaching as a profession.

2. I will not knowingly make any public statements that are untrue or misleading, or make false claims in any written documents relating to the coaching profession.

3. I will respect different approaches to coaching. I will honor the efforts and contributions of others and not misrepresent them as my own.

4. I will be aware of any issues that may potentially lead to the misuse of my influence by recognizing the nature of coaching and the way in which it may affect the lives of others.

5. I will at all times strive to recognize personal issues that may impair, conflict, or interfere with my coaching performance or my professional relationships. Whenever the facts and circumstances necessitate, I will promptly seek professional assistance and determine the action to be taken, including whether it is appropriate to suspend or terminate my coaching relationship(s).

6. As a trainer or supervisor of current and potential coaches, I will conduct myself in accordance with the ICF Code of Ethics in all training and supervisory situations.

7. I will conduct and report research with competence, honesty, and within recognized scientific standards. My research will be carried out with the necessary approval or consent from those involved and with an approach that will reasonably protect participants from any potential harm. All research efforts will be performed in a manner that complies with the laws of the country in which the research is conducted.

8. I will accurately create, maintain, store, and dispose of any records of work done in relation to the practice of coaching in a way that promotes confidentiality and complies with any applicable laws.

9. I will use ICF member contact information (e-mail addresses, telephone numbers, etc.) only in the manner and to the extent authorized by the ICF.

Professional Conduct with Clients

10. I will be responsible for setting clear, appropriate, and culturally sensitive boundaries that govern any physical contact that I may have with my clients.

11. I will not become sexually involved with any of my clients.

12. I will construct clear agreements with my clients and will honor all agreements made in the context of professional coaching relationships.

13. I will ensure that, prior to or at the initial session, my coaching client understands the nature of coaching, the bounds of confidentiality, financial arrangements, and other terms of the coaching agreement.

14. I will accurately identify my qualifications, expertise, and experience as a coach.

15. I will not intentionally mislead or make false claims about what my client will receive from the coaching process or from me as their coach.

16. I will not give my clients or prospective clients information or advice I know or believe to be misleading.

17. I will not knowingly exploit any aspect of the coach-client relationship for my personal, professional, or monetary advantage or benefit.

18. I will respect the client's right to terminate coaching at any point during the process. I will be alert to indications that the client is no longer benefiting from our coaching relationship.

19. If I believe the client would be better served by another coach, or by another resource, I will encourage the client to make a change.

20. I will suggest that my clients seek the services of other professionals when deemed appropriate or necessary.

21. I will take all reasonable steps to notify the appropriate authorities in the event a client discloses an intention to endanger self or others.

Confidentiality/Privacy

22. I will respect the confidentiality of my client's information, except as otherwise authorized by my client, or as required by law.

23. I will obtain agreement from my clients before releasing their names as clients or references, or any other client identifying information.

24. I will obtain agreement from the person being coached before releasing information to another person compensating me.

Conflicts of Interest

25. I will seek to avoid conflicts between my interests and the interests of my clients.

26. Whenever any actual conflict of interest or the potential for a conflict of interest arises, I will openly disclose it and fully discuss with my client how to deal with it in whatever way best serves my client.

27. I will disclose to my client all anticipated compensation from third parties that I may receive for referrals of that client.

28. I will only barter for services, goods, or other nonmonetary remuneration when it will not impair the coaching relationship.

APPENDIX 2

How to Find a *Christ-Centered* Coach

Process for Finding a *Christ-Centered* Coach

1. Get biographical information for at least three coaches.
2. Pay close attention to:
   - Coach certification (and the certifying organization)–ICF certification is the international standard for professionalism and ethics in coaching.
   - Coach training
   - Coaching experience
   - Christian confession and involvement
   - References

3. Ask for a sample coaching session. Pay attention to how well you connect and whether you think you could quickly build a trusting relationship. Note if the coach speaks readily of God and of personal faith.

Where to Find a Coach

The following Web sites can steer you to the coach who will serve you best:

www.coachfederation.org

The International Coach Federation maintains a referral service for their members. You can search on "Christian" to narrow the list.

www.thecolumbiapartnership.com

A collection of Christian coaches who have been selected to serve The Columbia Partnership customers.

www.valwoodcoaching.com

A collection of Christian coaches who have been selected to mentor coach students of Valwood coach training courses at Hollifield Leadership Center, Conover, North Carolina.

www.glcc.com

A collection of Christian coaches who have been selected to mentor coach students of GreenLake Coaching Center coach training courses at GreenLake Conference Center, GreenLake, Wisconsin.

www.christiancoaches.com

A collection of Christian coaches who are a part of Judy Santos's network.

ICF Certification Requirements

Associate Certified Coach (ACC) Requirements:

- 60 hours of coach-specific training
- 100 hours of client coaching experience—documented
- Attend ICF-sponsored educational teleforums

Professional Certified Coach (PCC) Requirements:

- 125 hours of coach-specific training
- 750 hours of client coaching experience—documented
- Coached or mentored by a MCC or PCC for minimum of ten hours over at least a three-month period

Master Certified Coach (MCC) Requirements:

- 200 hours of coach-specific training
- 2,500 hours of client coaching experience—documented
- Coached or mentored by a MCC or PCC for at least ten hours over at least a three-month period
- Documented contribution to coaching profession

Notes

Chapter 1: Why *Christ-Centered* Coaching?

[1]See Edward H. Hammett, *Spiritual Leadership in a Secular Age: Building Bridges Instead of Barriers* (St. Louis: Lake Hickory Resources, 2005).

[2]Edward H. Hammett, *The Gathered and Scattered Church: Equipping Believers for the 21st Century* (Macon, Ga.: Smyth & Helwys, 1999).

[3]Michael L. Simpson, *Permission Evangelism: When to Talk, When to Walk* (Colorado Springs: Cook Communication Ministries, 2003).

[4]Patricia M. Y. Chang, *Pulpit and Pew Research Reports: Assessing the Clergy Supply in the 21st Century* (Durham, N.C.: Duke Divinity School, 2004), 5.

[5]Dean R. Hoge and Jacqueline E. Wenger, *Experiences of Protestant Ministers Who Left Local Church Ministry* (Norfolk, Va.: Catholic University of America, 2003), also available at www.pulpitandpew.duke.edu/Hoge.pdf.

[6]Brian D. McLaren, *The Church on the Other Side* (Grand Rapids: Zondervan, 2003).

[7]Leonard Sweet, *Post-Modern Pilgrims: First-Century Passion for the 21st Century Church* (Nashville: Broadman & Holman, 2000).

[8]Topic "Church Attendance and the Bible," www.barna.org. Accessed 23 May 2005.

[9]Leith Anderson, *Leadership That Works: Hope and Direction for Church and Parachurch Leaders in Today's Complex World* (Minneapolis: Bethany House, 2002).

[10]A great book to help with vision casting is Andy Stanley, *Visioneering: God's Blueprint for Developing and Maintaining Vision* (Portland, Oreg.: Multnomah, 2003).

[11]Anderson, "Expectations–the Rules Are Changing," in *Leadership That Works,* 110–28.

[12]Chang, *Pulpit and Pew Research Reports.*

[13]George Bullard, *Pursuing the Full Kingdom Potential of Your Congregation* (St. Louis: Lake Hickory Resources, 2005) is a great book for orienting around vision and mission instead of management and programs.

[14]Coaching described throughout this book is as defined by the International Coach Federation (ICF). See Appendix 1.

[15]Bullard, *Pursuing the Full Kingdom Potential.*

[16]ICF is the largest non-profit professional association worldwide of personal and business coaches, with 8,366 members and more than 132 chapters in 34 countries.

[17]See ICF Competencies in Appendix 1 and Standards and Ethics of ICF in Appendix 2. Both are documented at www.coachfederation.org.

[18]Francine Russo, "Play of the Day," *Time* (25 September 2000).

[19]Kathryn Tyler, "Scoring Big in the Workplace," *HR Magazine* (June 2000).

[20]See ICF certification requirements in Appendix 2 and www.coachfederation.org.

Chapter 2: *Christ-Centered* Coaching

[1]See the ICF definition for coaching in Appendix 1, "The ICF Philosophy of Coaching."

[2]Laura Whitworth, Henry Kimsey-House, and Phil Sandahl, "Listening," in *Co-active Coaching: New Skills for Coaching People Toward Success in Work and Life* (Mountain View, Calif.: Davies-Black Publishing, 1998), 31–48.

[3]Thomas G. Crane, *The Heart of Coaching: Using Transformational Coaching to Create a High Performance Culture,* 2nd ed. (San Diego: FTA Press, 2002).

⁴Gary R. Collins, *Christian Coaching: Helping Others Turn Potential into Reality* (Colorado Springs: NavPress, 2001).

⁵Mary Beth O'Neill, "Developing a Strong Signature Presence," in *Executive Coaching with Backbone and Heart: A Systems Approach to Engaging Leaders with Their Challenges* (San Francisco: Jossey-Bass, 2000), 17–40.

⁶See ICF competencies in Appendix 1, "The ICF Philosophy of Coaching" and at www.coachfederation.org.

⁷I learned this from Dr. Anthony Grant, the founder and director of the world's first university-based Coaching Psychology Unit at the School of Psychology in the University of Sydney in Australia., www.psych.usyd.edu.au/psychcoach.

⁸Thomas G. Bandy, *Coaching Change–Breaking Down Resistance–Building Up Hope* (Nashville: Abingdon Press, 2000).

⁹Gary R. Collins, "What Is a Christian Coach?" in *Christian Coaching*, 13–26.

¹⁰With acknowledgment to Dr. Lee Smith, one of my coaches, for inspiration to link these tenets to Scripture. First presented at the ICF Prayer Breakfast, Vancouver, British Columbia, 2000.

Chapter 3: The Benefits of *Christ-Centered* Coaching

¹Patrick Lencioni, *Death by Meeting: A Leadership Fable....about Solving the Most Painful Problems in Business* (San Francisco: Jossey-Bass, 2004). This is a great book for making meetings more effective.

²Patrick Lencioni, *The Five Dysfunctions of a Team: A Leadership Fable* (San Francisco: Jossey-Bass, 2002). This is a great book to use when coaching teams.

³Laurie Beth Jones, *Jesus, Life Coach: Learn from the Best* (Nashville: Nelson, 2004). This is a great book about what it is like to experience the coaching of Jesus.

⁴Conrad Gempf, *Jesus Asked* (Grand Rapids: Zondervan, 2003). This book looks intently at the questions of Jesus.

Chapter 4: *Christ-Centered Coaching* Leverages Your Strengths

¹Marcus Buckingham and Donald O. Clifton, *Now, Discover Your Strengths* (New York: Free Press, 2001).

²Jerry L. Fletcher, *Patterns of High Performance: Discovering the Ways People Work Best* (San Francisco: Berrett-Koehler, 1993).

³The Highlands Ability Battery, www.highlandsprogram.com.

⁴Buckingham and Clifton, *Now, Discover Your Strengths*.

⁵Steve Moore, *The Dream Cycle: Leveraging the Power of Personal Growth* (Indianapolis: Wesleyan Publishing House, 2004).

Chapter 5: *Christ-Centered Coaching* Provides Clarity and Focus

¹Jerry L. Fletcher, *Patterns of High Performance: Discovering the Ways People Work Best* (San Francisco: Berrett-Koehler, 1993).

²From interview with Jerry Fletcher.

³Laurie Beth Jones, *The Path: Creating Your Mission Statement for Work and for Life* (New York: Hyperion, 1998).

⁴Steve Moore, *The Dream Cycle: Leveraging the Power of Personal Growth* (Indianapolis: Wesleyan, 2004). The book is all about realizing God-inspired dreams.

⁵Confidentiality has been protected in this story. Actually, multiple versions of this story have happened—more than you could imagine. I combined several stories to convey this to you, but each of the elements described here did happen as a result of coaching.

Chapter 7: *Christ-Centered* Coaching Catapults Learning

[1]I don't know where this model originated. I know I didn't invent it. A coaching colleague, Ray Lamb from the United Kingdom, introduced me to it.

[2]John J. Ratey, *A User's Guide to the Brain: Perception, Attention, and the Four Theaters of the Brain* (New York: Vintage Books, 2002).

[3]Ibid., 17.
[4]Ibid., 20.
[5]Ibid., 26.
[6]Ibid., 25.
[7]Ibid., 26.
[8]Ibid., 5.
[9]Ibid., 6.
[10]Ibid., 11.

[11]Malcolm Gladwell, *Blink: The Power of Thinking without Thinking* (New York: Little, Brown, 2005).

[12]Melissie Clemmons Rumizen, *The Complete Idiot's Guide to Knowledge Management* (New York: Penguin, Putnam, 2001), 85–96, 99–100.

Chapter 8: *Christ-Centered* Coaching Fosters Intentional Progress

[1]Reprinted with permission from Thomas G. Crane, with Lerissa Patrick, *The Heart of Coaching: Using Transformational Coaching to Create a High-Performance Culture,* rev. ed. (San Diego: FTA Press, 2001).

[2]David Allen, *Getting Things Done: The Art of Stress-free Productivity* (New York: Penguin Books, 2003).

[3]See Coach U Inc., "The Five S Model," *The Coach U Personal and Corporate Coach Training Handbook* (Hoboken, N.J.: John Wiley & Sons, 2005), 112.

[4]Ken Blanchard, *Lead Like Jesus* (San Diego: Oasis, 2004).

[5]Jim Horan, *The One Page Business Plan* (El Sobrante, Calif.: One Page Business Plan Company, 2004).

Chapter 9: *Christ-Centered* Coaching Rubs Off on Others

[1]My favorite leadership development tool is Legacy Leadership™ because it is developed with a coach approach. The designers, Dr. Lee Smith and Dr. Jeannine Sandstrom, are fine Christian women. I know because both have been my coaches at different points in time. www.coachworks.com.

[2]See www.thecolumbiapartnership.com for information on this.

Chapter 10: *Christ-Centered Coaching* Encourages God-Sized Goals

[1]Henry Blackaby and Claude King, *Experiencing God: Knowing and Doing His Will* (Nashville: LifeWay, 1990).

[2]John Ortberg, *If you Want to Walk on Water, You've Got to Get Out of the Boat* (Grand Rapids, Mich.: Zondervan, 2001).

Reaching People under 40 while Keeping People over 60

BY EDWARD H. HAMMETT WITH JAMES R. PIERCE

"Those who read this book and follow Hammett and Pierce's coaching will find a win-win approach to reaching both of the cultures present in today's world. This book should be on the desk of every pastor of an established church for the next two decades."

■ Bill Easum, Easum, Bandy & Associates

978-08272-32549

Recreating the Church

Leadership for the Postmodern Age

BY RICHARD L. HAMM

"Dick Hamm asks an essential–and deeply faithful–question of the church: Where are we going? Then, through analysis and insight into both past and future, and with an unwavering commitment to the mission of the church, Hamm points us in the right directions."

■ Wesley Granberg-Michaelson, General Secretary, Reformed Church in America

978-08272-32532

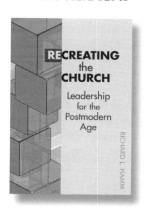

Pursuing the Full Kingdom Potential of Your Congregation

BY GEORGE W. BULLARD JR.

"If you want your church to mature and get beyond the preservation stage and to fulfill God's will for Kingdom growth, then study, read, and pray through this book."

■ Denton Lotz, General Secretary, Baptist World Alliance

978-08272-29846

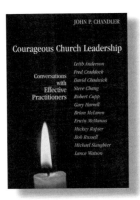

Courageous Church Leadership
Conversations with Effective Practitioners
BY JOHN P. CHANDLER

"Great leadership hinges primarily on one thing–finding the courage to be yourself. Chandler uncovers the stories of some who found that courage and became remarkable leaders."

■ Jim Henderson, executive director of Off-the-Map, former director of leadership development at Vineyard Community Church

978-08272-05062

The Heart of the Matter
Changing the World God's Way
BY CHARLES HALLEY

"With great insight and real world testing, Charlie Halley points out that personal transformation and congregational transformation are inseparable."

■ Don Cousins, congregational coach, former executive director of Willow Creek Community Church

978-08272-14521

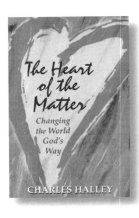

Enduring Connections
Creating a Preschool and Children's Ministry
BY JANICE HAYWOOD

Providing a thorough introduction to preschool and children's ministries, Janice Haywood addresses the questions a childhood minister faces and ways to answer them.

978-08272-08216